Whatever Happened to the Year of the Woman?

Whatever Happened to the Year of the Woman?

Why Women Still Aren't Making It to the Top in Politics

Amy H. Handlin, Ph.D.

Arden Press Inc.

Copyright © 1998 Arden Press, Inc.
All Rights Reserved

No part of this publication may be reproduced, stored in a retrieval system, or transmitted, in any form or by any means, electronic, mechanical, photocopying, recording, or otherwise, without the prior written permission of the publisher.

Library of Congress Cataloging-in-Publication Data

Handlin, Amy H., 1956-
    Whatever happened to the year of the woman?: why women still aren't making it to the top in politics/Amy H. Handlin.
      p. cm.
    Includes bibliographical references and index.
    ISBN 0-912869-22-4 (pbk.)
    1. Women in politics—United States.   2. Women politicians—United States.   3. Sex discrimination against women—United States.
    I. Title.
HQ1236.5.U6H35   1998
305.42'0973—dc21   98-9554
                                                                              CIP

Typography and interior design by Pearson Design.
Cover design by Bookends.

Published in the United States of America

Arden Press, Inc.
P.O. Box 418
Denver, CO 80201

Contents

List of Tables . . . . *viii*
Acknowledgements . . . . *ix*

Introduction:
What the Women Have to Say *1*

1 Running in Place:
 The Recent History of Women in Politics *7*

2 The Dual Life:
 Parenting Issues and the Mommy Track in Politics *19*
   Susan: A Precarious Balance. 19
   Family First 20
   Proving Their Mettle 25
   Rachel: The Mommy Trap 27
   The Mommy Track. 29
   Different Ladders. 34
   A Double Standard 37

3 "Our Dirty Little Secret":
 The Myth of Women's Solidarity *41*
   Carol: Crossing the Invisible Line 41
   "Letting Down Their Own Side" 43
   Where Are the Mentors?. 45
   "Queen Bees" 50
   "Like One of the Boys" 55
   Fundraising Revisited: Are Women
     Writing the Checks? 59
   Politicians with PMS. 62

v

4 Doing Good or Doing Favors:
   Motivations and Frustrations in Political Life *65*
   Maureen: Preserving a Personal Identity 65
   A Career—Or a Calling? 66
   The Politics of Power 70
   Why Do It? 73
   The "Old Boys' Network" 76
   A "Typical Woman" 82
   Structural Problems 86

5 Beyond the Battlefield:
   Challenging the Norms of Legislative Warfare *89*
   Barbara: "A Nice Do-Gooder Lady" 89
   Politics As Blood Sport 92
   Interactive Leaders 95
   "A Social Worker with a Little Power" 98
   "Not on a Pedestal" 100
   Partners in Change 104
   "We Just Work Harder!" 105
   The Ultimate Goal: Balance 108

6 Crashing the Parties:
   Of Business, Bosses, and Back Rooms *111*
   Laura: From Poster Girl to Pariah 111
   Diane: Who's Running the Show? 113
   Ladders or Anchors? 114
   "None of the Old Boys Were Interested" 116
   The Business of Politics 119
   Women's Solidarity vs. Party Unity 121
   "A Man without a Country" 127

7 No Cleavage during Speeches: The Do's and Don'ts
   of Appearance, Behavior, and Political Etiquette *131*
   Alison: It's All in the Eyes 132
   Do Clothes Make the Woman? 135
   Speaking Their Minds—Loudly 137
   "Do Not Cry. Ever." 141
   Mud and Blood: Should Women Give As
      Good As They Get? 142
   "People Will Assume You Couldn't Get a Babysitter" 146

8 *Not Just Another Yes Man:*
   Where Do We Go from Here? *149*

Appendix:
Women's PACs and Donor Networks *161*

Notes *169*
Bibliography *183*
Index *193*

Tables

Table 1.1.	Top 10 Legislatures for Women	*10*
Table 1.2	Percentages of Women in Elective Offices Before and Since the "Year of the Woman"	*13*
Table 3.1	Contributions to Female Legislative Candidates by Gender (1994-1995)	*61*
Table 4.1	A 10-Year "Voter Registration Gap"	*87*
Table 6.1	Women As Local Party Chairs	*124*
Table 8.1	1996 Presidential Election: Percent of Votes by Gender	*153*

Acknowledgements

I owe a debt of gratitude to the women who agreed to be interviewed for this book. Most are identified in these pages; some, at their own request, are not. But all gave generously of their time, energy, and insights. The distinctive voice of each enriched the whole beyond measure.

I would also like to thank a few individuals and groups for contributions above and beyond the call of duty. While I obtained lists of women officials from many sources, the Women's Campaign Fund and the National League of Cities were especially helpful with locating potential interviewees. The staff at the Center for the American Woman and Politics, the nation's most important repository of information about female elected officials, never failed to find answers to my many questions. My colleague Dr. Karen Schmelzkopf generously shared and helped to analyze a significant portion of the data in Chapter 6. Beverly Luck of the Monmouth County Library was endlessly resourceful in locating hard-to-find books and articles, while Rachel Gardner of the Monmouth

University Library patiently coached me through numerous database searches. I appreciate the early encouragement of another colleague, Dr. Guy Oakes, and the unflagging enthusiasm of my editor, Susan Conley of Arden Press, throughout all the arduous months of writing.

A special thank you to Fran Hanley, who gave unstintingly of her personal time to help make this book a reality; to Sara Biser; and to my colleagues Drs. Margaret Del Guercio and Barbara Andolsen for stalwart personal and professional support.

Central to this work, as to all that I do, are my husband David and my children Daniel and Rebecca. They give my life purpose while filling it with laughter and love.

Introduction:
What the Women Have to Say

In recent years, women have pushed open many doors to the political system. But in some ways, they seem perpetually stuck in the entryway. On most levels of elective office, their numbers continually inch forward. But progress is so slow that most newcomers are simply replacing others who depart. At the pinnacle of power—the U.S. Senate and the nation's governorships—the number of female pioneers has yet to reach a dozen. It seems that women are running faster and faster—just to stay even.

For at least 10 years, scholars have studied this problem; journalists have reported on it; women's groups have agonized over it. Indeed, just about every interested party has weighed in on the issue—except for the women who are most affected by it.

This book is about what they have to say. While it includes the perspectives of some of the few women who have made it to the top—governors, senators, and members of Congress—it is based primarily on interviews with those who are still climbing. As town council members, mayors, county commissioners, and state legislators, they describe firsthand what it is like for women to live a political life, at the grassroots level, in the 1990's. Their observations open a window onto the ways politics and public service are changing—and not changing—in America's towns, cities, counties, and states. Their descriptions are, of course, subjective—but that is the point. How political women construe their own experiences is a critical, and too often neglected, piece of the puzzle.

It is also a timely one. The United States has now moved well beyond 1992, christened the "Year of the Woman" by journalists who had never seen anything like it. Indeed, the events were historic: in that single, stunning election, more women won congressional contests than in the previous 20 years. Four new female senators vaulted into history, the most ever elected at once. Record

1

numbers of women snared seats in the state legislatures. Full equality, the pundits announced with confidence, was just around the corner.

Unfortunately, the promising prediction was never fulfilled. Only a handful of new women went to Washington in 1994 and 1996. As the decade wore on, state-level gains in female representation sputtered nearly to a halt. In retrospect, what women learned from the experience of 1992 was not how easy it had become to succeed in politics but how hard it still remained.

But despite the hardships of political life, many women persevere. That is because, as individuals and as a group, they believe that they matter: to their communities, to other women, to the political system, and to America.

A word about methodology.

My knowledge of the lives of women politicians comes not only from research but from living a political life myself. I have won four elections and served in public office (on my town council, as deputy mayor, and as a county commissioner) for more than a decade. This political experience makes me sensitive to the nuances of language that politicians use and alert to the questions raised by their behavior. At the same time, my training in marketing research enables me to judge where the narrow viewpoints of individuals intersect to create broader insights into groups. Together, these two perspectives—that of participant and that of observer—define the scope and approach of this book.

Marketing is about tapping into consumers' needs, desires, and perceptions, many of which are subconscious or difficult to articulate. For example, if I ask you why you bought a particular car, you're likely to cite its style, safety, or price. You probably won't say that you bought it to make a statement about your success. You won't admit that you wanted to defy the conventional standards of your workplace.

To give voice to these underlying factors, marketing researchers employ certain interview techniques. The techniques are designed to probe beneath the surface, drawing out the reasons for people's attitudes, behaviors, and beliefs. Much more than most research methods, "depth interviews" capture the unique world view of each subject; they enable her to express her own thoughts, in her own words, on her own terms. Research of this type can enrich the study of women in politics, which has been dominated by quantitative, impersonal survey techniques. As pointed out by political scientist Denise Baer, only qualitative and individualistic methods can illuminate "the experiential worlds which have meaning to women."[1] In simpler terms, the best way to understand how people see their own lives is to ask them.

This book is built around interviews with 50 officeholders from 22 states. The interview sessions sometimes seemed to take on a life of their own: not a few of the women unburdened themselves to me for over four hours at a stretch. Others called me months after our original discussion to expand on their thoughts or to contribute additional observations. Several requested anonymity, either in full or in connection with certain experiences. I selected some of these particularly revealing stories, with names and identifying details altered, to open or punctuate each chapter.

The interviews were far-ranging. I encouraged each woman to talk about her ambitions, motivations, and expectations in political life. Did she perceive differences between her experiences and those of the men she knew in politics? How would she describe her own leadership or management style? Does her gender matter to her constituents? We also explored some of the conventional wisdom about women in politics, such as the idea that most women, at least within the same party, can be depended on to help and support each other. Each participant answered the question: Why do you think there aren't more women in politics, especially at the highest levels?

It is important to note that this study was designed to be exploratory, not statistically determinative. I did not attempt to evaluate the current status of all political women or to forecast what will happen to them in the future. Instead, I set out to document what is happening now, to some of them, and to seek insights into how these women "make it"—or why they don't.

Certain patterns emerged from the interviews. I have tried to explain those patterns, using current scholarship not only about women in politics but also about women in corporate management—another traditionally male, high-stakes, and extremely competitive, if less public, milieu.

Demographically, the participants differ little from the profile of most female elected officials across the country. Most are or have been married, with at least one child. Their median age is approximately 48, and their children are most often over 12; 90% are white,

10% African-American. Almost all are college-educated, and their most common occupation is teacher. Nine are attorneys, though most of these do not maintain an active practice. I spoke to roughly equal numbers of Republicans and Democrats. There were no daughters of celebrities or national political figures, none with independent wealth or unusual visibility. In short, nothing about them was extraordinary—except what they were doing with their lives.

Despite widely differing ideologies, the women were all alike in their enthusiasm, openness, and willingness to take time out of extremely busy schedules to talk to me. In fact, most were fascinated to hear the stories of others, which I often shared with them after completing their interviews. In one way or another, they echoed the comment of Virginia State Senator L. Louise Lucas: "Just knowing that you've heard these things before—it validates my experience. I'm sane after all!" It was clear that they delighted in the notion of belonging to a community of women across the country—in contrast to the sense of isolation that they commonly experience at home.

Some readers may wonder why I chose to write much of this book in the third person, rarely drawing from my own experience. There are two reasons. First, I have not personally encountered all of the problems—or opportunities—discussed by those I interviewed. More importantly, my research training makes me wary of generalizing from any one case—especially my own.

That said, it is also true that this project is, at least in part, a personal quest. While I have been blessed with many supportive friends in political life, male and female, I also empathize with Senator Lucas. Having served for 8 of my 10 years in office as the lone woman on a governing body, I have long felt the hunger for women's company and community that the essayist Adrienne Rich described so well: "the desire for a context in which our own strivings will be amplified, quickened, lucidified, through those of our peers."[2]

I am proud to claim the women in this book as my peers.

***

It is important for the reader to begin with a general understanding of the recent history of women in politics. Even more critical than the history itself are the questions it raises: about the kind of women who run for office and about what happens when they get there.

This book is not intended to answer all the questions but to invigorate our struggle with them—and to remind us that these questions will help define the nature of American democracy for many years to come.

1
Running in Place:
The Recent History of Women in Politics

> *"A slow sort of country," said the Queen. "Now, here, you see, it takes all the running you can do, to keep in the same place. If you want to get somewhere else, you must run at least twice as fast as that!"*
>
> —Lewis Carroll, *Through the Looking Glass*

The face of American politics has changed. As recently as the 1970's, female elected officials were rare and remarkable. But today they seem an enduring presence, if still a small and scattered one.

Some of the statistics are impressive. In the two decades between 1973 and 1993, the proportion of women in state legislatures nearly quadrupled: from 5% to 20%. Among mayors of cities with populations over 30,000, the proportion of women soared from 1% to 18%. The 105th Congress, which took office in 1997, had over 40% more women than the 101st, seated in 1989.[1]

Most voters are now highly receptive to women candidates. This is true not only at the local level, where female officeholders have gained a stronger foothold, but in federal elections as well, where the electoral appeal of qualified women has long been known to match men's.[2] In general, women candidates benefit from the perception that they are more honest, trustworthy, and compassionate than their male counterparts.[3]

Both major political parties proudly trumpet their openness to female candidates. On both state and national levels, the parties even run special women's training sessions and outreach programs. Few party or elected officials would publicly disagree with the proposition that it is healthy for the country to have more women serving in government.

And it is clear that when they are elected, women make a difference. In the 103rd Congress (1993-1995), for example, women played a distinctive role in shaping and passing legislation, according to a three-year study by the Center for the American Woman and Politics at Rutgers University. Far from being limited to so-called "women's issues," their impact extended to such policy areas as international trade, crime, and gun control. For example, a bipartisan group of 20 congresswomen and female senators helped ensure that a ban on assault weapons was part of the 1994 Omnibus Crime Bill. When it came to the floor, the bill included restrictions on 19 types of semiautomatic assault weapons; it won the support of 40 out of 48 women in the House and 6 of the 7 women in the Senate. On other important legislation, such as the Family and Medical Leave Act (which shaped the nation's first guarantee of unpaid leave for workers who must deal with family or personal problems), the congresswomen as a group voted differently from their male colleagues. While half of the Republican women in the House supported the FMLA, only 27% of House G.O.P. men did; all of the Democratic congresswomen voted yes, but 13% of Democratic men voted no. Additionally, female lawmakers joined hands across parties to work on issues of particular concern to women: the bipartisan Women's Caucus introduced 70 bills in 1993 alone on matters such as women's health, domestic violence, and educational equity.[4]

On the state level, too, women officeholders translate their unique perspectives and life experiences into legislative action. In a 1991 study of the perceptions and attitudes of legislators across the country, women and men agreed that having females in the statehouse meant increased attention to how bills affect women, a larger number of bills dealing with women, and changes in the spending priorities of their state.[5]

***

All of this makes it particularly jarring to consider another set of statistics. Near the end of the twentieth century, the U.S. Congress remains nearly 90% male. Two-thirds of the women in the House of Representatives represent just seven states, which account for less than 40% of the population. Seven states have never sent a woman to the U.S. Senate or House. The 1996 election doubled the number of female governors—from one to two. (A third woman, Arizona Secretary of State Jane Dee Hull, was not elected to the office of governor but took over from Governor Fife Symington when he was convicted of fraud in 1997.)

Five years after the "Year of the Woman," the proportion of women state legislators just barely topped 21%. Women hold only 18% of seats in the state senates, which are more prestigious and usually more powerful than the lower legislative chambers.[6]

Change continues, but at a snail-like pace. At current rates of increase, say experts, it will take American women more than 400 years to achieve political parity.[7]

Such figures are especially stark when placed in international perspective. The United States trails most of the world's stable democracies in electing women to its national legislature. For example, Austria, Germany, and the Netherlands elect women in twice the proportion as the United States. While some democracies have still lower proportions of female representation (Belgium, France, Greece, Israel, Japan, and Malta), women in these countries did not even have the right to vote until the 1940's.[8]

Despite the dramatic gains of 1992, female members of the U.S. House of Representatives were barely numerous enough to hold their ground in the face of 1994's losses and retirements. When the polls closed in November 1996, only four new women were headed to the House. There was also some backsliding. In the "Year of the Woman," 39 female candidates ran for open seats, where the absence of an incumbent vastly improves the odds of winning; almost 60% of them (22 new congresswomen) emerged victorious. In 1996, only 28 women vied for open seats—and all but 5 of them lost.[9]

The proportion of women in the state legislatures had increased steadily during much of the 1980's. But as it leveled off and stagnated in the 1990's, momentum petered out. While the national press had been gleeful about women's prospects, its optimism sagged, too: in November 1995, the *Los Angeles Times* reported somberly that "the march toward parity had stalled."[10]

Moreover, a closer look at women in the statehouses yields some troubling insights. All state legislative bodies are not created equal; rather, they vary widely on measures of power and prestige. Based on relative levels of member compensation, staff budgets, and length of sessions (a surrogate measure of professionalism), the National Conference on State Legislatures divides them into three groups. Type 1 legislatures are full time, heavily staffed, and highly paid. Type 3 legislatures are part time, minimally staffed, and low paid. Type 2 are hybrids. Ranges can be enormous. For example, New York legislators (Type 1) receive a salary of $57,500 and a base allowance of $165,000 per year for staff, while their counterparts in Arkansas (Type 3) are paid $12,500 with an annual staff budget no higher than $13,800.[11]

The 10 legislatures with the nation's highest proportions of female representation are listed below: not one is a Type 1 body. Conversely, 4 of these top 10 are in the Type 3 category. It is hard to ignore this lopsidedness. Do women advance most where tangible rewards are least?

Table 1.1. Top 10 Legislatures for Women

State	% Women	Legislature Type
Washington	39.5	2
Nevada	34.9	3
Colorado	33.0	2
Arizona	30.0	2
Vermont	30.0	3
Oregon	30.0	2
New Hampshire	29.7	3
Maryland	28.7	2
Idaho	28.6	3
Kansas	27.9	2

Source: Fact Sheet, Center for the American Woman and Politics, National Information Bank on Women in Public Office, Rutgers University, August 1996.

Clearly, women are running on a very bumpy road; on some measures, they are virtually standing still. While their presence has increased markedly on the lower rungs of the political ladder, progress is uneven. And at the top, success disproportionately eludes them. Why?

In their search for answers, most researchers have looked to women's campaigns. The logic is straightforward: if women can't run competitive campaigns, they can't advance in politics. Indeed, most female candidates in the past faced major problems in such areas as fundraising and voter receptivity to women candidates. But much has changed.

Fundraising is a particularly important indicator. For better or worse, money is the *sine qua non* of politics, and the fundraising ability of women candidates is closely tied to their success. Throughout the 1970's and 1980's, female politicians regularly reported crippling difficulties with this part of the campaign process. And in the 1990's, some of the same problems persist—especially in garnering large individual contributions and support from powerful PAC's.[12] There remains a perception, true or not, that women must work harder to build the same war chests as men.

But there is little question that their work is showing results. Of the five women elected to the U.S. Senate in 1992, all but one raised more money than their (male) opponents. On the House level, studies of many types of races between 1976 and 1982 showed no significant gender-based funding differences.[13] In 1992, 48% of the 108 female candidates raised more money than their opponents.[14] And in state legislative contests, women candidates in some states now routinely out-raise and out-spend comparable men.

This is not to suggest that campaigns in general are easier to finance. On the contrary, the costs of all types of races have spiraled steadily upward for a decade or more. But the hardships of political fundraising seem, at least, more equitably distributed than in the past.

Another historical concern was voter hostility to women candidates, routinely documented by political scientists in the 1950's and 1960's. This hostility reflected traditional sex-role stereotyping (the notion that "women belong at home"), and it fell off as women entered the workforce in steadily increasing numbers. In 1970, 1975, and 1984, the Gallup Poll asked Americans whether they would vote for a qualified woman for Congress: the proportion answering "yes" rose from 84% to 91% over the 14-year period.[15] There may well be some residual anti-woman bias among portions of the electorate, but this is likely to be offset by pro-woman voting tendencies that emerged in the late 1980's and 1990's. Because women are drastically underrepresented in the traditional power structure, some voters apparently welcome them as fresh faces in a stale system.

On the state level, too, voter resistance to women has dropped off sharply. Studies of both primary and general elections in a variety of states show little or no difference in the proportion of votes received by men and women candidates, all else being equal. Even in states like Oklahoma and regions like the South, which have been among the slowest to elect female legislators, there is no apparent voter hostility. For example, those few female Oklahomans who do run for office not infrequently outpoll men.[16]

So, some of these older issues have been at least partially resolved. But newer ones have surfaced.

One contemporary issue is simply put: Where is the "new" political woman?

A quarter-century has passed since large numbers of women burst onto the electoral scene. America has since changed all around them. But female politicians, as a demographic group, have remained largely the same.

For example, because most women wait to run until their children are independent, female officeholders have consistently been older than men. This can be a serious limitation. For one thing, a late start means less time to build seniority. But it also means fewer opportunities to advance and, eventually, diminished stamina with which to pursue them.

While the majority of women legislators are now college-educated, they continue to hold fewer advanced degrees and to have less experience than men in business and the professions. Substantial numbers of female politicians list their primary occupations as homemaker, clerical worker, teacher, or nurse.[17] And there is no reason to expect sweeping change anytime soon: a 1994 survey of female and male executives and lawyers found that while 40% of the men had already considered running for office, 75% of the women had never thought about it.[18] So, for the foreseeable future, many women still must come from behind in building fundraising bases, influential networks, and the credibility they need to compete with well-connected, high-powered men.

This persistence of old trends seems strange because so much is new for the general population of American women. According to the U.S. Bureau of Labor Statistics, women now hold nearly half of all middle-management jobs, while mothers of preschool children are steadily flooding the full-time workplace. Women are entering such traditionally male professions as law and medicine at an unprecedented rate. In fact, the percentage of law degree recipients who are female nearly doubled between 1980 and 1990[19]—of particular significance to political women, since law has been a traditional springboard into elective office for men.

The failure of the political system to attract, or keep, a more diverse group of women is ominous. It is a hint of rigidity at the core, despite years of change at the margins.

There are other puzzles. Exactly what happened in 1992? Hailed as a tidal wave for women, the election of that year turned out to be an isolated swell.

How isolated? Compare the sharp spike in women's representation in Congress and the state legislatures between 1991 and 1993 (the outcome of the "Year of the Woman") to the sluggish rates of increase during the three election cycles that preceded and followed it:

Table 1.2. Percentages of Women in Elective Offices Before and Since the "Year of the Woman"

	Congress	State Legislature
1985	5%	15%
1987	5%	16%
1989	5%	17%
1991	6%	18%
1993	10%	21%
1995	10%	21%
1997	11%	21%

Source: Center for the American Woman and Politics, Eagleton Institute of Politics, Rutgers University.

Part of what made 1992 unique was the furor surrounding the unprecedented sexual harassment charges brought against Supreme Court nominee Clarence Thomas by a little-known law professor named Anita Hill. While Americans in general were split over the veracity of the charges, there is no question that millions of female television viewers were outraged by the powerfully sexist imagery: a Senate Judiciary Committee comprised entirely of men staring uncomprehendingly at Hill as she tried to describe a form of emotional and physical duress endured almost entirely by women. One national magazine bitingly remarked that the committee looked like "an aging former football team from a segregated school."[20] The editor of *Redbook* charged that Hill had been "gang-raped by the Senate."[21]

Other ingredients added to the pungent political mix of 1992, such as the House banking scandal, where it was revealed that some longtime representatives had repeatedly and brazenly bounced checks at the members' bank. Whether in response to this embarrassment or for other, coincidental reasons, a record number of congressmen (86) chose to retire or were redistricted out of their seats. Angry voters—especially female voters—made it clear that they expected immediate, visible change.

For the most part, they got it. To capitalize on these currents in public opinion, both political parties strongly encouraged women to run, especially for federal offices. What remains unclear is how much these efforts departed from "business as usual." The success of 1992 begs a question: How different are other years, in terms of encouraging women? What happens to them without the extraordinary circumstances that defined the "Year of the Woman"?

And a larger issue is raised by virtually all previous research, which has tended to focus heavily on the characteristics of women's campaigns and their electoral success rates. Studying women when they run tells us nothing about why they may choose not to run—or how they are dissuaded from running. These factors take on heightened importance when they affect women who have built substantial track records and are well positioned to bid for the most prestigious offices—but do not.

Why does this latter group matter? Because political women collectively cannot advance to the top without sufficient numbers ready and able to take advantage of every opportunity. In moving up the political ladder, women (like men) are impeded primarily by the paucity of open seats at the highest levels of office; regardless of gender, it is far more difficult to unseat an incumbent than to win an open seat. But when a seat does open, there must be one or more women willing to vie for it—and all too frequently, there are not. Still more worrisome is recent evidence that female legislators voluntarily relinquish their seats and retire from politics sooner than men.[22] It takes much effort to reach even the lowest rung of the electoral ladder; why, then, would these women jump off? This is a serious concern because women who leave politics are still extremely hard to replace.

Conventional wisdom holds that female candidates for state legislatures comprise a "farm team" of political leaders for the future. If so, the farm's productivity is inconsistent. In 1992, the "Year of the Woman," there was indeed a bumper crop of women running for state legislatures: 75% of the states had more than in the previous election cycle. But this kind of increase is exceptional. In 1988 and 1990, just over half the states had more women candidates than two years before. By 1994, only a third did.[23] Between 1994 and 1996, there was an absolute decline in the nation's total pool of female legislative candidates.[24]

Much hoopla greeted the women running for the U.S. House of Representatives in 1992—there were 108 of them, more than ever before. The national press excitedly declared that American politics had turned a corner: women would now skyrocket to parity. Hyperbole flowed freely even from cautious publications like *Business Week,* which crowed: "Washington is never going to be the same again."[25] It sounded too good to be true.

And it was. While the major parties have nominated more and more women to run for the U.S. House since 1992, the rate of increase has slowed, and the total number of female candidates remains underwhelming. In 1994, only 12% of all national candidates were female.[26] In 1996, the ratio of male to female House candidates was still no better than two-to-one.

On the other hand, it has often been suggested that women are disproportionately shunted into so-called "sacrificial lamb" candidacies.[27] These are situations where the presence of an entrenched incumbent or other circumstances make it almost impossible to win.

Some believe that women simply lack the level of personal ambition that drives men to seek, and to win, high elective office.[28] Perhaps, they suggest, the proverbial "fire in the belly" is dampened in women by socialization, stereotyping, family constraints, or some combination of these and other factors.

But there is another possibility. Political women's ambition may differ from men's because it is shaped by particular motivations and goals—not because it is weaker. For example, surveys have shown that most women politicians run for office because they want to improve their communities, defined narrowly (their towns) or broadly (the country). They are less attracted by opportunities to attain personal visibility or establish business contacts, which can motivate men.[29] A male politician may be faster to jump at the chance to run for higher office because, win or lose, he views the campaign itself as a way to expand his horizons. For his female colleague, the perceived risks may be different. She could lose what matters most to her: the ability to bring about change.

Another constraint on ambition is the degree to which it is encouraged (or discouraged) by others, particularly political party leaders or other elites, and how much that matters. Some research suggests that women's political career moves are much more heavily influenced than men's by such external factors.[30] Among advocates for women in politics, there is increasing recognition that ambition can be reinforced through supportive feedback: for example, a recent national training seminar for female officeholders featured a workshop entitled "Ambition Is Not a Dirty Word."

The issue is not whether political women have ambition—but whether, and when, they choose to act on it. Among the thousands of women who have won their local political spurs, there are clearly growing numbers who aspire to higher office. But aspiring is not the same as running—or winning. Part of the reason for women's disproportionate lack of success at winning high-level offices is that potentially strong women are withholding their hats from the ring. Or, they are running at inopportune times and under adverse political circumstances. Why?

The question may also be framed another way. Political life is more than the periodic waging of campaigns; it is a process of living and working day to day, in election season and out. What are the forces inherent in this life that are driving the choices of women within it? Do these forces reinforce the glass ceiling even as they open doors beneath it?

***

Women in corporate management are frustrated, too. As repeatedly documented by the U.S. Department of Labor's Glass Ceiling Commission and independent researchers, the progress of managerial women halts abruptly at the executive suite.[31] In education and training, corporate women and men are approaching equality; in attaining positions of leadership, they remain far apart. How far? As of October 1996, women held only 2% of the top five jobs at the nation's 500 largest companies.[32]

Management experts have identified certain conditions that impede the advancement of women in corporations. For example, an absence of mentoring opportunities hits women harder than men. This is because male managers tend to have informal networks that provide contacts, feedback, and career guidance. Excluded from these "old boys' networks," women need mentors to provide alternative sources of support.[33]

Additionally, some experts say, women may be disadvantaged in environments that emphasize short-term performance or where there is unusually fierce competition among top leadership.[34] Ambitious women become frustrated and unproductive when they find themselves in dead-end, unchallenging jobs, where they are more likely than men to be stuck.

Parallels between corporate and political environments abound. By its very nature, the business of politics is focused on the short term. There is cutthroat competition among political leaders for visibility and power. Most women have poor prospects for advancement. And formalized mentoring is virtually nonexistent; even informal relationships among fellow politicians rarely transcend opportunism or convenience.

It is also revealing that in both corporations and politics, the same explanation is usually given for women's absence at the top: they haven't been in the pipeline long enough. But some observers have begun to question how much is enough. Snaps Eleanor Petersen, first woman chair of the Illinois Fair Employment Practices Commission:

> It takes time, we're told, to rise through the pipeline in any profession or organization. How much time? Women have been pushing hard against the glass ceiling on business promotions for at least 30 years, but 30 years is not enough. . . .The suffragist movement began its struggle for equal political rights more than a century ago, and we now have 7 women senators [sic] out of 100. Are we supposed to be proud of that achievement? Wouldn't shame be a more appropriate reaction? The pipeline argument is a sham and a disgrace.[35]

A recent study of 461 top corporate women showed that many of them agree. While most male chief executives continue to argue that there are not enough women with sufficient experience to reach the top, less than half of the women surveyed shared this belief.[36] Moreover, the current status of women in corporate America makes it clear that change will not come easily or soon.

Despite much public hand-wringing over the years, the glass ceiling shows nary a scratch. In 1992, a second federal commission was convened to study the problem. Its report, issued in November 1995, revealed that at least 95% of senior managers of Fortune 500 and Fortune 1000 companies are still men—despite the fact that 57%

of their workers are now women. "The 'glass ceiling' is a concept that betrays America's most cherished principles," the report stated.[37] But the "betrayal" goes on.

***

There is another parallel—between women in politics and women in non-elective state and local government jobs. Sociologist Catherine White Berheide showed that the percentage of such women in the lowest-paying employment categories is four times higher than that of men (five times higher than that of white men). This increasing feminization of the lower ranks has only served to highlight, not to change, the paucity of females above. Berheide describes this phenomenon—of women entering government service at the bottom and simply getting stuck there—as a "sticky floor."[38]

***

This, then, is the story of both a glass ceiling and a sticky floor: an amalgam of factors that impede political women's rise to the top, even as female officeholders accumulate in greater and greater numbers on the bottom. Importantly, it is not a story about discrimination per se: on the contrary, among this group there were mercifully few reports of outright discriminatory actions or statements. Rather, it is about what happens when women encounter the behavioral norms and expectations of a world that remains largely alien to them.

In their recent book, *Women and Politics Worldwide*, authors Barbara Nelson and Najma Chowdhury put this alienation in global perspective:

> Our point is not that women are never powerful or that they never enjoy political equality with men. Women frequently exercise political power in a particular arena, and in many situations their political activism is distinctive or unopposed. Rather, our point is that these situations are always exceptional in some manner. . . . Men of any (national) group are more able to be active in politics than can the women of their group.[39]

British author Elizabeth Vallance was more blunt: "Where the power is, women are not."[40]

2
The Dual Life: Parenting Issues and the Mommy Track in Politics

*At a very early period she had apprehended instinctively the dual life—
the outward existence which conforms, the inward life which questions.*
—Kate Chopin, *The Awakening*

Susan: A Precarious Balance

In her cavernous office, Susan appears even smaller than she is. A diminutive woman in her early forties, she steps quickly from behind the imposing executive desk to greet a visitor. "Let's talk over here," she says cheerfully, indicating a couple of comfortable armchairs. "It's a lot more homey."

As mayor of the fastest growing city in her state, Susan has considerable visibility and clout. She is no stranger to fiduciary responsibility and authority, having given up a promising career in corporate finance to move to this area and raise her children. Her springboard into politics was a large and important community association that looked to Susan for leadership on zoning, transportation, and other local issues. The group's faith in her paid off; over time, she not only helped achieve its objectives but also ousted the former mayor who had opposed them.

The mayor who likes things to be homey, it turns out, also differs in other ways from the popular image of a single-minded political leader. For all her obvious strengths as a person and as a politician, Susan is acutely aware of what she sees as a weakness. "It's the balancing act—I can't seem to get it right," she says, shaking her head. "I really enjoy what I do, and I do it well. I was top vote-getter in every precinct in the city. But I feel stressed out all the time because of my kids. I live with a constant sense of guilt. . . . How could anyone not be affected by that?"

In addressing tough municipal issues, like her plan to revitalize a blighted downtown, Susan is firm and decisive. But when she talks about her family, her tone turns anxious and confused. "I'm always wondering whether I have my priorities straight. Am I a terrible mother because I missed my son's band concert to attend a public hearing? Am I a terrible mayor because I left a council meeting to get to a parent-teacher conference?"

She is particularly concerned about her daughter. The teenager has become increasingly resentful of Susan's absences from home—and even more of the fact that as mayor she is always the center of attention.

"One way I've tried to help her feel better about my career is by taking her with me to political events. I wanted her to meet other people who are involved in the process; I hoped she'd see that it's exciting and important, not just a time-consuming job that her friends' mothers don't have to do." But the strategy backfired. "Instead of enjoying the events, she just got angry because everyone wanted to talk to me and not to her. I'm especially worried about that. I know it's hard for her to build up her own self-esteem when she's always being upstaged by her mother."

Susan is convinced that women bring unique strengths and an important perspective to politics, and she wants to continue her own career. But for the foreseeable future, her ambitions are on hold.

"Will I run for higher office? It all depends on what happens first in my life," she predicts. "Either my kids will grow up okay, or I'll burn out—and it might be both."

Family First

Most of the politicians I interviewed were also mothers. About a third had children under 18 still living at home.

A unique kind of challenge faces these women. They are elected to serve others—and without exception, every one was passionately committed to doing so. But meeting the needs of a large constituency takes extremely long hours, not to mention an emotional toll. Strictly political responsibilities—fundraising, attending partisan events, and so on—add to the burden. Small wonder, then, that many of these mothers share a common set of anxieties about shortchanging their children. They also share a strong tendency to put children and families first whenever possible in their political careers.

Political scientists have believed for some time that family responsibilities weigh more heavily on mothers than on fathers in elective office. There is evidence for this both in where women serve and in when women run.

Across states, female legislators tend to cluster in districts that are close to the state capital. This suggests a concern about travel and a desire to avoid long absences from home. Similarly, when asked about the factors that determine when (or if) they run, far more women than men cite parenting considerations as extremely influential.[1]

Mayor Susan Bass Levin of Cherry Hill, New Jersey typifies this pattern. In a state dominated by strong Republican women (Christine Whitman is one of only three female governors), and where 89% of mayors are male, she is one of a tiny handful of women cited by major newspapers as potential Democratic statewide candidates. Will she run for higher office? "Well, my second child has one more year to go in high school—then I'll be ready to consider it," she says. Her perspective is striking because it clearly places family responsibilities above political opportunities.

These issues may be critical at key decision points in an officeholder's career. But do they play a role in her daily life?

The politicians I interviewed not only answered emphatically "yes"; they seemed incredulous that anyone could think otherwise. Theirs was a new twist on the old feminist slogan "The personal is political."

Their perspectives as caregivers, whether currently or in the past, clearly influenced their priorities and decisions. For example, educational improvements were a common goal: one tenacious officeholder spent 13 years lobbying for full-day kindergartens. "I knew from my own experience with kids that early childhood education is critical to later development," reflects Councilwoman Marcia Weaver of Jackson, Mississippi. "So I wouldn't let go." Environmental and land use issues were frequently viewed through the prism of family safety and health. Even traffic regulations could be approached this way:

while serving on the governing body of Springfield, Illinois, Gwenn Klingler voted to restrict parking on residential streets not because of congestion but to protect neighborhood children.

Nearly every local official I interviewed cited her town's "quality of life" as her top priority. What does that phrase mean? In a virtual chorus, almost all echoed the response of Mayor Alice Schlenker of Lake Oswego, Oregon: "It means my main focus is on children and families—education, recreational facilities, security on our streets." When Viola Baskerville ran for city council in Richmond, Virginia, she decided to focus on what she called the "kitchen table" realities of family life: "While the guys were all talking about 'economic revitalization,' I used the theme 'Our neighborhoods are our future.' It brought things back to the home, to what's around us that's important. It was very basic and simple, and all voters could relate to it."

As a town councilwoman in Elsmere, Delaware, State Senator Patricia Blevins—whose two children were under six at the time—was acutely aware of the scarcity of good child care. When she became mayor, she lowered municipal registration fees to encourage the start-up of more small day care facilities. Running for the legislature a year later, she found this to be an effective issue: "My opponent had opposed day care tax credits. We were able to draw a real contrast between my record and his." Like Blevins, officeholders at every level of government unfailingly linked child care accessibility to job growth and prosperity.

Women may be discouraged from explicitly linking their perspectives to their legislative goals, however. "People told me it was a mistake to focus so much on children in my campaign for the legislature in 1992, because children don't vote," recalled Judge Bettieanne Hart, a former Georgia state legislator. "But the problems of children in rural areas were my impetus for running—my campaign theme was 'For the Sake of the Children'—and voters understood that I was the only candidate talking about the future. By the end of the campaign, everyone was talking about children!"

When U. S. Representative Zoe Lofgren filed the forms required by the State of California to declare her candidacy, she described her job in the space provided as "mother." Officials informed her that "mother" was not a recognized occupation. "They're telling me motherhood is not a job," Lofgren retorted. "As any mother will tell you, it is a job, 24 hours a day. It seems to me that being a parent is probably the most important job to the future of our country. If the law says that doesn't count, the law is wrong."[2]

While most of the mothers I interviewed were married, none had relinquished the role of primary parent and manager of the home. Few advocated doing so either. "The woman is still the core of the family, and I don't think that's going to change," comments Christina Selin, a councilwoman in New Rochelle, New York. "I always felt that raising my son the right way was my most important contribution to society." Illinois State Representative Gwenn Klingler tries to turn a constraint into an opportunity: while she believes that few mothers with young children will ever be able to manage officeholding above the local level, she encourages them to put their community rootedness to good use. "I want them to understand that they can build a record and name recognition while staying close to home. That will give them a leg up on the competition for higher offices later."

But most of the mothers I spoke to would not concede so much ground. Given supportive spouses and the right kind of office (some legislatures, for example, are in session for less than the length of the school year), they insisted that all options were—or should be—open, even to those with preschoolers. These women were not militant, and none of them trivialized the motherhood dilemma. They knew all too well that public scrutiny and unpredictable hours only complicate the issues that confront any working parent. But they strongly believed that women should be trusted to make their own decisions about what was best for their families. And having made such decisions, they tried not to look back.

U. S. Representative Tillie Fowler of Florida, for example, had two pre-teens at home when she launched her political career. "I was so concerned about the whole thing," she recalls. "I went to a pediatrician to talk about what it would do to my children. I talked to friends who had teenagers. It's part of being a mother. I don't think men worry about that. My friends who have teenagers said, 'Do it now; there will be more problems when they are teenagers. Get on into it. It'll be better.' And they were right."[3]

A few officeholders made a point of telling me that they had continued running their homes exactly as they did before entering politics. They were proud of managing their public duties without disrupting their families. But they were not superwomen. They had simply resigned themselves quietly, and not always happily, to paying the price of added anxiety and stress. "When there's a snowstorm and the schools close, I'm still the one who ends up staying home with our kids," one mayor sighed. "It doesn't matter that I'm also the mayor who's accountable to the whole town for getting the schools open again."

Even when family issues weighed heavily on their minds, most of the officeholders were determined to excel in spite of these concerns—and sometimes because of them. To Councilwoman Judy Ferguson Shaw, it was important to improve youth facilities in Berkeley, Missouri; what better way to accomplish this goal than to establish the town's first Youth Commission, with Shaw's 9- and 11-year-old children as members? Indiana State Representative Mary Kay Budak described why she relentlessly pursued legislation extending hospital insurance coverage for maternity patients, from one day to two. "My daughter developed toxemia (a condition characterized by high blood pressure and other dangers) at the point of giving birth," she explained. "Her husband has to travel a lot; had he not been there on that first night at home, she would have just passed out on the floor, alone with a one-day-old baby." U.S. Representative Marge Roukema of New Jersey specializes in health issues at the federal level. When asked why, she points out simply that she lost a 17-year-old child to leukemia; for her, it is reason enough.[4]

Also, some women are speaking out for more family-friendly elective institutions. Late-night debates, unscheduled sessions, last-minute meetings—all make it increasingly difficult for a committed family man *or* woman to participate in government. Notes U.S. Senator Kay Bailey Hutchison: "Some of us joke that what we really need are wives, because it's very difficult to do what you have to do as a senator and also take care of your family. We need to address family life and the pace of work here."[5] According to former Representative Lynn Schenk, women are not alone in their dissatisfaction with the overheated congressional schedule: "The younger men who are used to working with women, who have been raised by feminist mothers or married to women who have careers—they want some of the same things."[6]

When Virginia's Delegate Shirley Cooper was first elected to a county board, she pointed out to her colleagues that their practice of holding meetings to sell bonds at 7:00 A.M. precluded many members of the public from participating—not to mention her own problems in arranging supervision for two preschoolers at that hour. Rebuffed at first, she persisted: "The guys on the board told me that this was the way it was done, that I just had to get there. So, I brought my kids along and set up a playpen in the county chambers. That made my point. The meetings were changed to nighttime."

Proving Their Mettle

What psychologists call the "achievement motive"—a relentless drive to perform despite personal obstacles—goes hand in hand with the pride of winning election to public office. But there was more in these women's stories than simply a desire to do their best. Many of them felt a need to compensate for the undeniable fact that their attentions were divided—or to "prove" to male colleagues that they were capable of doing it all. In her experience as a legislator, commented Georgia's Judge Bettieanne Hart, she found that "men have credibility just by virtue of having been elected. . . . Women have to earn it." Connecticut State Representative Claudia Powers described how "a lot of women work extra hard to show that they're serious legislators—not just moms doing politics in between trips to the mall." Another legislator described this punishing routine:

> It's a solid three-hour drive between my house and the state capital. During the legislative session, we frequently have meetings that go until 1:00 or 2:00 in the morning. The guys don't care because they just stay over in a hotel. But when I ran for this office, I made a promise to my kids—that no matter what, I'd always be here to have breakfast with them and help them get ready for school. I refuse to break that promise. So, when we have those meetings, I get in my car at 2:00 A.M. and come back home at dawn. I'm a wreck. But I won't leave the meetings early, or ask for them to be changed. I have to show the guys that I have as much stamina as they do, and then some.

Political mothers are not alone in this. Many female executives also report that they must work harder to prove themselves, while male colleagues seem to command automatic respect.[7]

There appears to be more than just perception at work. In a recent study of almost 800 American executives with comparable levels of commitment to their careers, women with preschoolers were found to receive lower merit raises than men with children the same age.[8] In another study, male managers characterized the work-home relationship as "instrumental" in their success; managerial women experienced it as "conflicting."[9]

In the eyes of Susan and others, the political world demands still more of its women. Even when their credibility has been proven at the ballot box, it remains tenuous with other politicians. At considerable cost, they must continually reaffirm it.

Many mothers with political ambitions simply avoid these issues, at least temporarily; they postpone running for office until their children are grown. The continuing age disparity between women and men in elective office suggests that this approach is still the most common. Alternatively, some mothers seek only low-pressure positions close to home. Their dilemma is captured in the pithy comment of Judy Knudson, first and only woman ever elected to the Board of Supervisors of James City County, Virginia: "The glass ceiling is: who's going to take the kids to the soccer game?"

There is a pattern created by these coping strategies. Even when highly ambitious, women with parenting responsibilities run for higher office only when they believe it will not adversely affect their children—not necessarily at the first, or best, opportunity for advancement. They often postpone running for office, and then run at the local level to be close to home. And once in office, they feel pressured to prove themselves to male colleagues, yet another challenge to be tackled while serving their constituencies and managing their families.

This pattern has a variety of career consequences for women. None of them is trivial, or readily overcome. As observed by political scientist Marcia Manning Lee:

> Because of children, women may fail to gain the experience in their twenties, thirties and early forties that their male counterparts are acquiring. When, at last, they are free, they may lack the political knowhow and connections to effectively compete. . . .In short, most men interested in politics get a head start and it is very difficult for women to catch up.[10]

What is notable about this comment is that it was written in 1976. Two decades have passed, but the only change in Lee's picture is that a few more women, like Susan, now defy conventional wisdom and run for office while their children are still young. And on top of all the usual stresses of political life, they are confronting that most contemporary of women's issues: burnout.

For all that, these women and others like them are still succeeding—if the measure of success is an individual's ability to hold on to a current seat. Very few of the officeholders I interviewed had lost a reelection bid. Overall, women incumbents at various levels of office are no less formidable vote-getters than men. And in general, public opinion remains highly favorable toward women in politics, clearly a collective stamp of approval for the jobs they do.

But there are different criteria for judging the success of political women as a group. As noted earlier, women cannot advance toward parity without increasing numbers of candidates tossing their hats into every promising ring. Of course, the decision to run for office on any level is a highly personal one. But internal decision-making rarely occurs in a vacuum; in politics, it is subject to a variety of external constraints. Two common constraints, for example, are the individual's party support and the strength of a candidate's fundraising base.

There is no obvious reason why such constraints should affect women and men differently. After all, once established in office, politicians nowadays compete on equal footing for party support and campaign funding.

Or do they?

Rachel: The Mommy Trap

Election day is always special in Rachel's family, whether she is on the ballot or not. Her children—each born during one of her reelection campaigns—have accompanied her since babyhood to rallies and get-out-the-vote events. To them, elections mean excitement, anticipation, and the chance to be part of a process that their mother always told them was wonderful.

But Rachel is no longer so sure that the process is wonderful.

On the face of it, she is a highly skilled, successful politician. She began her public career early, taking on substantial community involvement even as she and her husband settled into their first home. Despite a daily two-hour commute to her job, she participated almost every night in meetings and activities of various issue-advocacy groups—because she loved it. "I was exhausted most of the time, but exhilarated, too," she remembers of those early days. And her husband was extremely supportive of her work.

Rachel quickly rose to leadership positions in several prestigious organizations and was often their spokesperson in the local press. Eventually, her high profile caught the attention of local party leaders, who offered her a spot on their city council ticket.

She was thrilled at the chance to run for office. "I had always thought it was something I'd like to do. I had no family or friends in politics, so I didn't really understand how the system worked. But I had achieved so much as a community activist that I was sure I could succeed at this, too."

And succeed she did, for over a decade. Rachel won election, and re-election, to the city council by unprecedented margins. Ambitious and eager to move up, she later sought and won the mayor's seat. Regional newspapers consistently praised her work, as did many citizens' groups.

She and her husband started their family during these years, too. Rachel was convinced that family life could, and should, be compatible with political life. "I made a point of bringing my children to community events, picnics, pancake breakfasts, wherever it was appropriate. Since I had every intention of staying in politics and moving up as they got older, I wanted the people and the activities to seem completely natural to them from the start."

Motherhood also informed her decision-making, she believes. "My kids made me much more sensitive to issues like child abuse and public health. I think that being a mother makes me a more well-rounded public servant."

Her children adjusted to their mother's schedule in political life—but Rachel also found it necessary to adjust her schedule to them. "I realized that I had to set some clear priorities and make some compromises, as I guess all working mothers do," she acknowledges with a smile. "I was determined not to shortchange either my responsibilities as a mother or my job as an elected official. But there are just 24 hours in a day, so something had to give. What I did was attend fewer purely ceremonial events like parades and partisan functions that I wasn't directly involved with, like fundraisers for other politicians. Or, I would show up for just a short time, enough—I thought—to show my support and still get home to my kids.

"Within my community and the party organization, everyone knew that I was cutting back on these things—I never tried to keep it a secret. Not that I could have fooled people anyway. I was the only elected official with a young family, and I realize now that I stuck out like a sore thumb."

After her children started school, an unexpected retirement produced an open seat in the state senate. Child care was a less pressing issue now than it had been for years, and Rachel jumped at the chance to run.

"I honestly believed that I had a lot to offer the district and the state. And after so many successful campaigns during the most demanding years of my life, I felt sure that I was ready to make this run."

But community and party leaders felt differently. "It wasn't until I asked for their support to run for the senate that I realized how they viewed me: as someone who did very well in local office but who wasn't 'committed' enough to move up. What mattered were appearances, not results. Despite my vote totals and years of accomplishment, I got trashed because I hadn't shown my face, or hadn't stayed long enough, at every conceivable ribbon-cutting and pancake breakfast, and apparently I had raised eyebrows by leaving a lot of these events early. Basically, I couldn't get the support I needed because of the tradeoffs I had made in order to care for my kids."

Rachel is careful to point out that she does not support special advantages for women in politics. "But I also believe that good people shouldn't be penalized for being mothers. I think that grappling with all those issues I had to confront as a parent—lack of child care, education problems, and the rest—would have made me a better state legislator, not a less 'committed' one."

The Mommy Track

To the women I interviewed, it was clear that the paths of women and men diverge at the fork of parenthood. Of course, some male politicians may accommodate their family needs in much the same ways as women do. But if this is so, few women seem to be aware of it.

Rachel was not alone in her experience of conflict between family and political roles. A four-term legislator, denied party support to run for U.S. Congress, believed this was partly because she had spent so much time caring for her elderly mother. Another had carried a beeper so that her children could reach her in an emergency, only to learn that male colleagues derided her for it. "It was perfectly acceptable for lawyers to carry a beeper for their clients, or doctors for their patients—but not mothers for their kids." One woman felt that she was left off the invitation list for get-togethers with important political contributors "because people assume I'm too involved with my kids to be interested."

Sometimes it seems that women's parenting decisions are used against them no matter what they do. As 1992 congressional candidate Patricia Garamendi told *Business Week,* when she approached political action committees, "The last question always was: 'What will you do about your children?' Having a 6-year-old daughter gives them an excuse to turn me down."[11] On the other hand, when former Democratic Congresswoman Blanche Lambert Lincoln announced in 1995 that she would not seek reelection because she was pregnant with twins, her decision was promptly ridiculed by a prominent national G.O.P. official. According to the *Washington Post,* he asserted that Lincoln's pregnancy was just "an excuse."[12] (Being childless offers no protection either: Mary Sue Terry, who ran for governor of Virginia in 1993, was denigrated for *not* having a family.)

The key question raised here is not whether women with family responsibilities can manage political careers. Despite the difficulties, some obviously can and do. The question concerns the short-term choices and tradeoffs made by such women. Can these choices have unintended long-term effects?

More specifically: Is there a "mommy track" in politics?

In 1989, management consultant Felice Schwartz ignited a firestorm when she recommended, in the highly influential *Harvard Business Review,* that companies divide their women workers into two groups: those whose work came first ("career-primary") and those who put families ahead of it ("career-and-family"). The first group could then be offered the same opportunities as men, the second, shunted off onto what the media dubbed the "mommy track." With less challenging assignments and more flexible schedules, most "mommy trackers" would forfeit any chance to reach the top.

According to Schwartz, however, they—and their employers—would be happier, or at least better off, for having eliminated the work-family conflict.

Immediately, debate about the mommy track exploded—*Harvard Business Review* published 32 pages of letters to the editor solely on that subject—and has raged ever since. Is it discriminatory, or simply realistic? Is it better for women, or just cheaper for their employers? Why did Schwartz assume that only mothers, not fathers, need help in accommodating family needs? Several years later, the only certainty is that the mommy track has become a common, and openly acknowledged, business phenomenon.[13]

The political "mommy track" is a close cousin to the corporate one. Women are no longer routinely barred from entering the system, or overtly prevented from moving up, but those with significant family responsibilities may be steered, subtly but firmly, onto a lower orbit. To be sure, they can enjoy long and satisfying careers on that orbit. Should they try to advance, however, they may confront special obstacles—both perceptual (the belief that they aren't sufficiently "committed") and real (limited access to money and support). Commissioner Sandra Miller of Bucks County, Pennsylvania, who spent years as a Democratic party leader before running for office, doesn't need convincing: "A woman may be removed from the short list of potential candidates because the decision-makers know she has significant family responsibilities," she reports, "and they won't even discuss the problem with her."

Another Pennsylvanian, Chester County Commissioner Karen Martynick, knows that such things happen in the Republican party, too—because they happened to her. "Even when I ran on the county level in 1991, there were comments about how I could do this with two kids. My younger child was already 16 when I entered the Republican primary for Congress in 1995, but that didn't make a difference. People repeatedly expressed doubts about how I could handle it with a family."

Such doubts may also hobble women who pursue high-level political appointments. One study of female appointees in the Carter and Reagan administrations found that half were childless—compared to fewer than one-tenth of Carter's male appointees and one-fifth of Reagan's. As pointed out by political scientist Susan Carroll, who authored the study, "Those responsible for making appointments may also apply a double standard, viewing women who have children as likely to have less time to devote to their jobs while making no such judgments about men who have children."[14]

There has been much progress on this front since the 1980's; for example, the Clinton administration appointed Carol Browner, mother of one child under 10, as chief administrator of the Environmental Protection Agency. It has often been suggested, however, that U.S. Attorney General Janet Reno was chosen partly because she was childless. This meant that she could not be criticized for improper child care arrangements, which doomed President Clinton's two earlier female nominees to the same post. The "Nannygate" scandal embarrassed the White House and badly tarnished both Zoe Baird, a respected attorney who had hired an undocumented alien to watch her children and failed to pay the woman's Social Security taxes, and Kimba Wood, a federal judge who also hired an alien (though Wood violated no laws). It did not, however, affect any of the president's male nominees with small children, as none of them were questioned about babysitting

Of course, a mommy track is not necessarily coercive. In the business world, many women on such a track have clearly made an informed choice to pursue their careers at a slower pace. For example, some female professionals at large law and accounting firms voluntarily postpone the reviews that lead to promotion and partnership. Also, it is not uncommon for female scholars at elite universities to extend the probationary period that precedes their evaluation for tenure.

From a corporation's perspective, accommodating the short-term needs of these women makes good business sense. Some of the best managerial talent is female. And experience has shown that valuable women executives may leave if forced to conform to traditional corporate behavioral norms—particularly the pattern of unvarying career focus over time and inflexible criteria for defining "commitment."

But there is a crucial difference between business and politics in this regard. To the extent that a mommy track exists in politics, it is not openly acknowledged: party leaders and political colleagues do not explain it, then offer a "choice." Instead, women like Rachel simply find themselves relegated to a lower trajectory for reasons they do not understand—until it is too late to do anything about them. For women like this, the mommy "track" becomes a mommy "trap."

They are trapped because of another difference between the boardroom and the "smoke-filled room." The typical corporate promotion timetable is fairly predictable. But political advancement is highly opportunistic; good chances occur erratically and unexpectedly. If a female politician, otherwise ready to run for higher office, is held to a mommy track by denials of funding or support, she may not get a second chance. Or, worse, she may not want one. "This is it for me," said one local officeholder who was exploring opportunities to run for higher office. "I've spent ten years juggling my family responsibilities to do a good job in this office. If people still think I'm not seasoned enough to move up, then I think it's time for me to move out."

Despite such differences, there is a key similarity between business and politics that helps explain why mommy tracks have developed—and why women have difficulty getting to the top—in both. Management scholars call it "organizational culture": a set of assumptions, beliefs, meanings, and values that are shared by most participants. Culture gives rise to behavioral norms and expectations. Implicitly but rigidly, it establishes the judgment criteria that are used to measure commitment to the organization, loyalty, and worthiness.

Through most of the twentieth century, the traditional cultures of business and politics were hospitable only to men—specifically, men with wives who took care of their homes and children. These men could devote endless hours, at virtually any time of the day or night, to whatever activities were deemed appropriate by the organization. Women with family responsibilities were not accommodated in any way; of course, for the most part, there were none to accommodate.

Some political scientists have suggested that women are still ignored and kept down because of a male conspiracy against them. But why bother to conspire? Men in political or corporate power have never needed elaborate efforts to thwart women: the organizational culture does it for them. As writer Terri Apter observes in her book *Working Women Don't Have Wives:* "The idea of a conspiracy against women . . . in many ways *underestimates* the obstacles to equality in the workplace. It presents obstacles to women's equality as requiring some special effort, some distinctive intention. . . . Instead, what occurs is an opening of opportunities to women within organizations which are persistently male in orientation and assumptions and procedure."[15]

Political scientist Susan Gluck Mezey puts it this way: "The number of women in office does not appear to be a reflection of purposeful discrimination against women, but rather a function of the normal business of politics."[16] Reflecting on the norms of this "business," Mayor Levin of Cherry Hill, New Jersey notes that prospective candidates for county offices are routinely told they'll have to campaign full-time from April to November. "I'm not sure whether that's really necessary for the campaign. . . . [I]t may just be put out there as the way people are expected to demonstrate their commitment and loyalty to the party. But it's certainly an obstacle to a woman with young children."

This is not to deny the well-documented history of sex discrimination that has further inhibited the rise of both business and political women. But the lessening of discrimination in recent years has not resulted in equality. Neither Rachel nor her counterparts experienced problems *because they are women;* they experienced problems because, as women, they were responsible for providing nurturance and support to others. In politics, these are liabilities—nothing less, nothing more.

Different Ladders

The mommy track in politics developed as a way to modify the organizational culture without really changing it. The result: women can now more easily get a toehold at the bottom, but it remains as difficult as ever for them to climb to the top.

How does this happen?

For one thing, the ladder itself is different. It may rise to the same height as the traditional ladder, but it starts at a lower base—and has extra rungs.

It is described by many political women—and not exclusively those with family obligations—who believe they must start at the bottom and run for every consecutive level of public office (preferably party offices, too) if they wish to move up. The expectations for men, they complain, are different. Men are commonly encouraged either to skip rungs (by "leapfrogging" from local office into Congress, for example) or to start their elective careers closer to the top. "I see it all the time," New Mexico State Representative Mimi Stewart observes with obvious irritation. "These young men just waltz into important positions—we women have to prove ourselves over and over in community work and party work before we have enough credibility to run."

"Showing that you're an ambitious woman can be a problem for people," said Pennsylvania's Karen Martynick:

> When I entered the congressional primary, some people told me that I was very young and I should "wait my turn" (I'm 43). One older woman said, "The state representative in my district is in her 70's. She'll be retiring soon. . . . You can take her seat." Meanwhile, I was opposed by a younger man who had gotten into the state senate in only 3 years. There were people who believed that he should get the nomination ahead of me and I should "work my way up"—even though I've been in politics for 15 years.

There is some objective data to support the notion of women patiently (or impatiently) "waiting their turns." In 1983, the Center for the American Woman and Politics (CAWP) at Rutgers University published an extensive study of the career paths of political women. It showed that a higher proportion of female than male legislators had held elective or appointive offices prior to their current ones (despite the fact that women got a much later start in politics). For example, female state senators were more likely than their male colleagues to have served in the lower legislative chamber. More women than men in state, county, and municipal offices had previously held at least one government appointment. Additionally, more women than men had worked on other political campaigns or on the staff of another public official before running for office.[17]

Similar results emerged from a more limited 1991 study of legislators in four states (Tennessee, Pennsylvania, Vermont, and Washington). Again, a higher proportion of women than men had served in both appointed offices and political party offices before their election to the legislature.[18]

Several other women with ambitions to run for higher office also told me with some bitterness that they'd been admonished by other politicians to "wait your turn"—in other words, to step out of the way of other eligible candidates. For one thing, they believed, men routinely ignore such niceties and simply run whenever they are ready. For another, as one mayor put it, "They make political advancement seem like catching a bus; all I have to do is wait for the next one. But I'm already a lot older than most of the other elected officials in my area; so this bus may come only once in my political lifetime. If I miss it, there's no other way to get where I want to go." Along the same lines, both Democratic U.S. Senator Patty Murray and Republican Congresswoman Sue Kelly were branded as upstarts when they announced their intentions to run; it is clear that neither would now hold federal office if they had deferred to other, better-established contenders. Worse, New Mexico's Mimi Stewart believes that the waiting game dampens initiative: "I think you lose your independence and aggressiveness if all you do is wait."

At any rate, it seems clear that women perceive a need to be prepared and seasoned for elective office in a way that men do not. What remains unclear is where this perception originates. It may be internal, driven by psychological factors (insecurity, lack of self-confidence) or practical ones (fewer fundraising contacts, less political knowhow). Or, it may be external—a set of expectations and standards perpetuated by party elites, colleagues, community leaders, or the electorate. Wherever it comes from, it colors the beliefs of women who have won races large and small. Shaking her head over the paucity of women running in her state, Virginia State Senator L. Louise Lucas laments: "We're constantly wondering, 'Am I really ready to do this? Do I know enough? Can I put enough time into it?' When a man runs, he just feels like he *deserves* to win." While Maryland's State Delegate Cheryl Kagan, at the age of 35, is one of her state's youngest legislators, she still wonders at "the men who've run for the legislature at the age of 23. I can't imagine having had the gall to do that!" Councilwoman Adele Smith of Ogden, Utah lifted a strand of her hair to show me its color: "See this gray? It's a real asset for me. People can see that I have plenty of life experience. When younger women talk to me about running for office, I advise them to wait."

A Double Standard

There is another striking facet of the picture. Asked in Rutgers' CAWP study about the influence of various factors on their decisions to run for office, women were far more likely than men to rate their prior political experience as very important.[19] We do not know what factors particularly influence men, but it is apparent that men believe other professional or personal experiences can adequately establish their credibility as political candidates.

Women who do not share this belief are sometimes indignant about it. This indignation came across in one woman's description of the selection of a U. S. Senate nominee by the state leaders of her party:

> It came down to two people, a woman and a man. I thought the woman was terrific: a lawyer with a lot of strong local experience. The man had run for Senate before, but he hadn't done anything in our state, wasn't even a resident—he was moving here just to run again. They decided to endorse him, of course. I'm sure if it had been the other way around—if his only experience was on the local level—they would have said it was much more important to have a community base than to be a former Senate candidate. What a double standard!

The notion of a double standard ("Women need experience, but men don't") also cropped up occasionally in descriptions of male opponents. Women officeholders who were well past 50 took umbrage at being challenged by 20-something men. A typical comment was, "At his age, I would never have been so arrogant! But these hotshot young guys. People tell them they can do anything—and they believe it!" Ironically, being challenged by young and inexperienced candidates pays a backhanded compliment to these women; it suggests in some cases that better-established politicians felt it was too risky to run against them. But that doesn't change the ubiquitous perception voiced by Virginia's Delegate Shirley Cooper, who after 15 years in the legislature still believes "we always have to be two times as good and three times as prepared" to compete, both on the campaign trail and in office.

Whether perceptual or real, the mommy track in politics intersects with and exacerbates the problems caused by more general parenting issues.

For one thing, it slows the progress of women who already enter politics later than men because of family needs. When these women aim for the top, they have farther to go as well as a shorter time to get there.

It can also act as a brake on political ambition. Studies have shown that ambition in women is most strongly correlated with age: older officeholders are less motivated to move up. But the data also link low ambition to perceived lack of political opportunity.[20] While this perception may certainly be based on objective factors, such as domination of the electoral district by voters of the opposing party, it may have a subjective component as well—rooted in a politician's beliefs about what doors are, and are not, likely to be open to her.

Ultimately, these problems can combine to create a pink collar ghetto of "women's seats": offices to which women are routinely nominated and elected but which offer little power and a narrow range of policy impact.

They can also slow the pace of change. Political scientists and women's advocates are unanimous in the belief that the more women run, the more women will win—on all levels. But getting more women to run means expanding the pool of quality candidates, and the combined effects of the issues discussed in this chapter are to further restrict it.

Most observers look to the country's first large crop of female lawyers and businesswomen to yield the "political woman of the future." She will, at last, be competitive with men on every measure: education, training, occupational skills, status, and savvy.

But female professionals commonly choose to establish their careers first and start their families later . . . and later. While the average childbearing age is up for all American women, it is especially high among those in this group.

This means that the window of political opportunity for the female candidate of the future will be even smaller than in the past—unless she finds new ways of coping with parenting and mommy track issues. The only alternative is a female candidate pool increasingly limited either to those who happen to bear their children at a relatively young age or to those who are childless.

Clearly, the better option is for women to develop strategies that will enable them to be both good mothers and effective politicians—without wearing themselves out in the process. But how? There is no book on the subject. There is no course called "Parenting for Politicians 101."

The most logical (and often, the only) source of help for women in politics is other women in politics. Because they have "been there," because they have either learned the ropes or found ways around them, more senior political women offer a wealth of understanding and support to their junior colleagues. At least this is the conventional wisdom.

The next chapter will explore whether it is true.

3
"Our Dirty Little Secret": The Myth of Women's Solidarity

"Women shouldn't be fighting each other over the crumbs, but working together to get the whole cake."
—Commissioner Karen Martynick

Carol: Crossing the Invisible Line

While she does not seem embittered by her experiences, Carol is clearly disappointed by some of the women she has encountered in politics. The walls of her comfortable den are covered with plaques and mementoes of her many years of advocacy for women—an ironic counterpoint to the story she tells.

Carol first won public recognition as the founder of her city's innovative domestic violence shelter. It took years of effort to raise both the money and the governmental consciousness that were needed to establish the center, and Carol, a survivor of domestic abuse herself, is justly proud. She makes a point of praising the dozens of other women from organizations like the League of Women Voters who helped her. "Looking back, it was probably the most positive and energizing experience of my life," she recalls fondly. "We all shared a vision and a goal; there was no competition among us. No one had a hidden agenda. I think part of the problem I had later was that my expectations of solidarity among women were so high after that."

Five years after the shelter opened, Carol decided to run for a seat on the all-male city council. "I saw that all my work in the community could be undone by budget cuts at City Hall. So I decided—it's time for someone with my priorities to get in there." She had been active for years in political party networks, working for other candidates and helping to organize fundraising events. "Up until that time, I had never thought of running myself. But I thought I had the right contacts and a pretty high public profile. Most importantly, I was confident that the women in the party would support me—and there were so many of them that we'd be unstoppable!"

She was wrong.

"I learned that there's this invisible line you cross when you decide to run for office. Before, you're just one among many other community or party volunteers doing things that nobody else wants to do. Then all of a sudden you're competing for this position that's very desirable, and some people look at you differently. They assume that you're only interested in power and glory. Before, you were like them; now you seem very threatening."

She continues, "I was able to take most of that in stride, because I understood that a lot of grassroots activists don't trust politicians in general. What really bothered me, though, was when I learned that several key women officials in my party were working against me. They said that I didn't deserve a council seat because I hadn't worked hard enough for the party—in other words, I hadn't done the same things they did. Some told me that I had to 'wait my turn,' because I was younger than the men who also wanted the seat. A few were downright catty: professionally I'm a writer, and when I heard them referring to me as 'Lady Hemingway,' I knew it wasn't a compliment."

Most disturbing to Carol was that these women were unmoved by her passionate commitment to issues like domestic violence. "I certainly wasn't one-dimensional; I made it clear that other aspects of the city's quality of life were very important to me, too. But I was the only one talking about problems of particular concern to women. And it just didn't matter.

"I know now that I was naive," she admits with a rueful smile. "I was aware that most of the female party officials had longstanding relationships with the other candidates. I guess I was idealistic enough to believe that they'd get excited about the prospect of having a woman there for the first time; but the only thing they seemed excited about was how much trouble it caused them when I had the nerve to come forward."

Carol persevered and won the election anyway. Now in her second term, she has consolidated her political strength by building a new coalition of nonpartisan activists and those few party stalwarts who did support her.

"The most important thing to me is that I've helped to secure the future of domestic violence treatment and prevention programs in this city," she emphasizes. "Unfortunately, along the way I learned that in politics, women often don't support other women: it's our dirty little secret."

As a postscript to this story, Carol told me that she was actively considering a run for the state legislature. When she approached an influential community leader to ask for his support, he laughed at her: "You must be nuts—even some of the women in town aren't behind you!" Carol's reaction: "I felt like saying, 'So what else is new?' But I didn't. I'd rather have him believe that women are a solid bloc of support for one another; that perception might help some other female candidate in the future."

"Letting Down Their Own Side"

Across the bounds of regions and political parties, I found a gaping hole in the fabric of support for many women. Conventional wisdom, as well as common sense, suggests that female politicians should find a solid base among others of their gender—not only as a source of votes but especially as a wellspring of guidance and encouragement from those who have preceded them. Certainly there are shared concerns, life experiences, and aspirations that define what it means to be female in America. For at least two decades, women have waited for that mutual understanding to flower into political advocacy.

Many are still waiting. Too often, the landscape of women's support for other women is less a garden than a desert. As *New York Times* columnist William Safire commented after the 1990 election cycle, a disappointing one for women on the federal level: "Women of every political stripe—at home and around the world—are letting down their own sexual side by not demanding more female candidates and by not supporting them when they run. . . . The reason . . . is a dismaying lack of assertiveness of group identity."[1]

There are important exceptions. Many women running for national office in 1992 enjoyed unprecedented success in mobilizing other women. More generally, the past decade has seen the growth and steady development of nearly 60 women's political action committees (PACs) and donor networks (a list of all these organizations is provided at the end of this book).

Four major national women's PACs are currently active. All of them blossomed during 1992, though the seeds had been planted years before. The bipartisan Women's Campaign Fund (WCF) and National Women's Political Caucus (NWPC) began raising money as early as the mid-1970's, while EMILY's List (Democratic women only) first endorsed candidates in 1986. Only the WISH List (Republican women only) was actually a product of the Year of the Woman, though many of its early supporters had previously donated to WCF. Each of these organizations is a serious political player, with its own distinctive appeal.

WCF, America's oldest non-party-affiliated women's political committee, has always supported exclusively pro-choice female candidates with money, training, and advocacy in Washington. During the 1994 election cycle, WCF supported 176 candidates with more than $760,000 in cash and technical assistance. Over a 20-year period, as its literature states, "WCF has nurtured thousands of America's most talented women candidates, sustaining them throughout their political careers—over 1,300 total."[2]

Through its educational arm, the Women's Campaign Research Fund, WCF has also launched a highly visible challenge to the defeatist view that all politicians are alike. As part of "Women Leaders for Change," a national voter education campaign, WCRF sponsored advertisements in major women's magazines during 1996. Each posed the question: "Who needs women in office?" Citing the accomplishments of female officeholders in enhancing the lives of women throughout America, the ads declared in letters as bold as the group's ambitions: "WE DO!"

The NWPC prides itself on an extensive grassroots network of state and local chapters, which help to identify and support women running for office as well as those seeking appointment to policy-making posts. "We put women in their place . . . for a Change" asserts its membership brochure. While NWPC has also supported men committed to its legislative goals, its primary focus is women: more than 2500 current or potential female candidates took part in its training programs during 1993-1994 alone.[3]

EMILY's List (the acronym stands for "Early Money Is Like Yeast") was initiated in 1985 to support female Democrats in national races. In 1988, the group backed 9 House candidates; by 1992, its list had grown to 44. Members are asked to write checks directly to endorsed candidates; in a practice called "bundling," the PAC then collects and disburses these funds. The WISH List (Women in the Senate and House), founded in 1992 to advance pro-choice Republican women, also adopted the bundling method.[4] By its fifth anniversary in 1997, the group could celebrate a 50% increase in WISH-endorsed members of Congress.

More recently, significant numbers of women have banded together to support female candidates in their own states. Some of these localized networks are party-affiliated and are discussed in Chapter 6. Among the bipartisan state organizations, Virginia's Make Women Count (MWC) is a particularly successful example. When it was founded by a small group of civic activists in 1993, Virginia ranked 43rd in the nation in the number of women serving in its legislature. Three years later, intensive recruitment, training, and fundraising by MWC on the local level had helped elect 5 new women and reelect 16 more. In addition to its campaign-related activities, MWC has also lobbied effectively for the Virginia Women's Agenda, a broad set of economic, legal, and family policy goals established by its board of directors and supported by all of its endorsed candidates.[5]

It would be nearly impossible to overstate the importance of such efforts to the long-term advancement of gender equity. The new support structures built from scratch by these organizations have literally altered the political landscape. But all women's PACs and advocacy groups must take a broad view; by definition, they must try to make impersonal forms of support—usually dollars and campaign training—available to as many worthy candidates as they can identify. The *particular* needs of individual women in their day-to-day political lives must be met in other ways. Unfortunately, those needs are not often being met by other women.

Where Are the Mentors?

One of the lessons of the civil rights movement is that making it illegal to keep people out of institutions doesn't mean they'll get in. A similar truism applies to women in politics: while they have finally established a voice, that doesn't ensure it will be listened to.

Getting listened to in the raucous, noisy world of politics is no small challenge, and it is unrealistic to assume that newcomers of either gender will overcome that challenge right away. Learning the ropes—developing alliances, deciphering the power structure, mastering legislative skills—takes time. And it takes help.

Men have always had help, both formal and informal. First, they have had career training. In law and business, the traditional springboards for male candidates, many have become highly proficient in advocacy and negotiating skills long before running for office. Second, they have benefited from the support and camaraderie provided by informal networks and from the guidance of political veterans who take rookies under their wing. These sponsors are popularly known as "mentors."

Research has shown that in informal interactions, people are more comfortable associating with others who are like them. This birds-of-a-feather tendency, as much as (if not more than) deliberate exclusion, helps explain why women in corporations and in politics tend to be absent from men's unstructured networks and groups— what many of my interviewees called "the boys' club."[6] Chapter 4 will take a closer look at the workings of these groups.

The inaccessibility of most support networks to women in male-dominated organizations makes mentors particularly important to them. This point was first articulated by management scholar Rosabeth Kanter in her groundbreaking 1977 book *Men and Women of the Corporation*. When there is a severe imbalance between members of different social categories (e.g., sex or race), Kanter argued, those in the minority experience unique "token dynamics"—that is, performance pressures and standards that are applied only to them.[7] (It is worth noting Kanter's definition of a "skewed group," in which token dynamics are most likely to flourish: an organization with a ratio of minority to majority members of approximately 15 to 85. As of 1996, there were 23 state legislatures with ratios of women to men either lower or only marginally higher than this benchmark.)

To overcome these token dynamics and scale the walls, women need guidance, encouragement, and training. In the absence of supportive networks, these must be provided by individuals—preferably experienced climbers.

Also, research on mentoring suggests that it need not emanate from those at the very pinnacle of success in order to be effective. While a mentor may lack the power to link his or her protégé with the most important people in the organization, that mentor can still offer coaching and simple friendship in an environment that is otherwise treacherous and viciously competitive.[8]

Given the robust potential of mentoring to help women advance in political life, I was surprised and disappointed to find that it is far from the norm. Only six of the women I interviewed could cite a particular person (other than a relative or personal friend who was not experienced in politics) as having guided or "looked out" for them throughout their political careers. Of those, only three of the mentors were female. (An additional 10 women characterized another female officeholder as a role model. However, they had enjoyed only minimal, if any, personal contact with her.)

But almost everyone was easily able to identify areas where a mentor could have given them a leg up (or prevented them from stumbling). These areas fell into three categories: personal, political, and professional.

The three mentoring categories are intertwined, according to Jo Ann Boscia, Council President in Lakewood, Ohio. In her additional role as president of Women in Municipal Government, a subsidiary organization of the National League of Cities, Boscia discusses such concerns with female officeholders from around the country. "Getting elected is a lot like becoming a parent," she observes. "You decide you want to do it, you run and you win, and then you say, 'Now what?' Being in public office isn't just a job; it's a whole way of life." On a personal note, Boscia adds: "It's always made me very sad that there was no woman in my community who took me under her wing and helped me figure it all out."

Personal mentoring, for these women, implied help with the perennial balancing act. This was most often on the wish list of mothers with dependent children, who share a special challenge when they serve in public office. "Lots of us don't need to learn how to do a brochure," commented Mayor Rose Krasnow of Rockville, Maryland. The mother of two young teenagers, she did not have a mentor and has tried to fill in the gap by attending women's campaign training schools. While these can be very helpful, she says, "they ignore the issues of personal conflict that are really critical to women in politics. Where we could use guidance and moral support is in dealing with issues of balance, how to maintain our family lives, things like that."

Extraordinary demands on personal time are only part of the problem. There is also immense emotional pressure when political mothers are torn between the needs of their families and their constituents. Too, public scrutiny can create unanticipated problems and tensions in the home. Some of the women had been dismayed about their families' reaction to negative publicity. "When the going gets rough," reported one councilwoman, "my husband feels a need to get going, usually to visit relatives in another town—and he insists on taking the kids to shield them, too. I don't like it, but he says it's the only way he can handle feeling so put upon and powerless."

Dress and deportment are significant personal issues, too. In campaigns and out, female officeholders are judged by cultural norms of attractiveness and appropriateness. (This topic is addressed in Chapter 7.) The arbiters of those standards are other women. Thus, women are in a unique position to help each other develop personal styles that are practical and acceptable—as well as photogenic.

Political mentoring means help in navigating the reefs and shoals of campaigning. Particularly for a first-time candidate, the array of skills to be mastered is dizzying: from fundraising to public speaking to handling the press. Additionally, an experienced mentor can make introductions, help build alliances, and steer the neophyte toward reliable people and important issues. When the mentor is well placed and respected, he or she can also help establish a candidate's credibility through public endorsements and private recommendations.

Professional mentoring smooths the path that officeholders must follow to do their jobs. In every elective office, from town halls to the U.S. Congress, there are unwritten rules and standards of behavior, as well as "tricks of the trade" that can make the difference between success and failure. For obvious reasons, these are best transmitted by a supportive ally with personal knowledge of the pitfalls and a commitment to helping the newcomer avoid them.

Why, then, the dearth of mentors for female politicians? Among men, lack of empathy or of experience with close platonic relationships may reasonably justify a failure to reach out. But how to explain this behavior among other women?

Experts on mentoring seem stumped by this question. "Shared femininity is a gift women can give to each other. Yet some women shun such generosity," wrote Joan Jeruchim and Pat Shapiro in their book *Women, Mentoring and Success*.[9] It is particularly baffling because a woman who does help another can derive important benefits for herself. As the magazine *Executive Female* advises its high-powered readers: "We may . . . fail to realize how mentoring can further the mentor's own career. Cultivating the career of a promising young executive, for instance, can get the mentor favorable notice, too—as a talent scout who not only can pick 'em but knows how to groom her discoveries for the big time."[10]

There appears to be a consensus among political women about what is going on. A big part of the problem, of course, is simple lack of energy and time. "It's so difficult, so time-consuming for us to climb the ladder that we tend to lose our focus on how important it is to bring other women along," reflected Commissioner Karen Martynick of Chester County, Pennsylvania. One veteran legislator put it this way:

> If we don't set priorities in our lives, we can't function. Our responsibilities to our families and our constituents come first, though there are certainly some of us who believe that our responsibility to help other women comes right after that. The problem is, taking care of those first-priority things takes every waking hour of every day. Even for those of us who really want to be mentors, it's just impossible to add another burden. When am I supposed to show the ropes to another woman? In the middle of the night?

But equally harried businesswomen have shown that where there is a will, there is a way. For example, when the corporate women's group at Banker's Trust Company sponsored a program of mentoring breakfasts, the organizers were overwhelmed with female bankers eager to make the time to participate. At one San Francisco law firm, the female attorneys decided to defy sexual stereotypes and offer mentoring teas. Again, there was an enormous response.[11] For the woman who cannot set aside even enough time to share a sandwich, there are mentoring opportunities in cyberspace: the accounting firm Ernst and Young uses its internal computer network to create connections between women with flexible work arrangements.[12]

It is never easy to be a trailblazer, perhaps least so in the face of unrelenting public scrutiny. For the women who made up America's first sizable wave of female politicians—running for office in the late 1970's and 1980's—survival skills had to come first. Until very recently, their total numbers were small, their influence limited, and their long-term viability unstable. It would have been counterproductive for those women, at that time, to put themselves at risk in order to help others.

Still, the historical perspective does not entirely explain current realities. Surely enough women have amassed enough strength by now to be able to share some.

Unfortunately, many still don't. But political women can only help themselves, their parties, and the political process by making mentoring a priority instead of an afterthought. For one thing, a mentoring program is self-perpetuating: those who owe their success in some part to a mentor will be on the lookout for their own protégés. In addition, it is a valuable tool for candidate recruitment and a symbol of commitment to diversity and inclusiveness.

"Queen Bees"

Claudia Powers is one of the younger women in the Connecticut legislature, first elected in 1992. Although she worked her way up through Republican Women's Clubs, she was not among those who identified a female mentor. Reflecting on her experience with other women since entering the statehouse, she offered:

> There are really two groups of women in the legislature, the newer and younger ones like me and the older generation who have been there since the days when it was much more of a men's club. I think that it was a lot tougher for those original women legislators to establish their credibility and get things done, and they did it pretty much on their own. So I guess I can understand why many of them don't try to be mentors for the newer women. No one ever did it for them, and it just never became one of their priorities.

Others were less charitable. One state senator described how she got her chance to run as a result of her visibility on another female senator's campaign. "But that doesn't mean she helped me personally. She didn't open one door for me; she didn't introduce me to one person. In fact, she sat on the party leadership committee that decided whether they'd endorse me, and hers was the only vote I couldn't count on."

A city councilwoman who was the second female ever elected to that post had this to say about the first: "There was a lot of tension between us. . . . She didn't like my barging in on her territory. It seemed like she saw herself as 'Queen of the Council.'"

New York Assemblywoman Susan John tells of "senior women in the legislature who have blocked my advancement." Referring to a committee appointment she especially wanted, John is certain that she was nixed by the committee's chairwoman: "She's a lawyer, too, and I think she was threatened by me." The word *threatened* came up often. Mayor Karen Anderson of Minnetonka, Minnesota chose it, too:

> In my experience working with women elected officials on the state and national levels, I've seen women deliberately working against other women. It took a tremendous amount of effort for those few women in power to get there, and when they feel threatened by women coming up in the next wave, I've sometimes seen them trash the newcomers.

Commissioner Karen Martynick points out that political women in her area have had limited opportunities, and so they tend to fight each other for the few public or party offices traditionally made available to them. "These positions aren't stepping stones. They're not really important; they're just crumbs. Women shouldn't be fighting one another for the crumbs; we should be working together to get the whole cake."

Jeruchim and Shapiro place such observations in a broader context. "Those women who've made it into the top rungs but don't help other women are called queen bees. If they've succeeded on their own, despite prejudice and chauvinism, they reason, why can't others? Rather than helping young women move up, the queen bee is threatened by bright young women and resents that they are given opportunities she never had."[13]

It does not seem only a matter of feeling threatened. Often an element of political risk is associated with supporting or helping other women—if only because they are often opposed by better-established men. When Commissioner Sandra Miller of Bucks County,

Pennsylvania ran in a primary for the statewide office of auditor general, "I was disappointed at how many women in leadership roles would not support me. I think that's because they were protecting themselves. . . . I wasn't the state party's endorsed candidate, and they would have been taking a risk by being out front for me."

Stories like Miller's underscore another point brought up by Jeruchim and Shapiro: "Others may see these women as firmly established in their high-level positions, but often they feel insecure. Their minority status and lack of power breed insecurity. . . . "[14] This sheds light on an observation made by Indiana Representative Vaneta Becker about the senior women in her party's legislative caucus: "They tend to be the ones who are least often willing to buck the leadership. I guess they feel they have the most to lose."

Like a family secret, the queen bee phenomenon is rarely exposed in public. For that reason, occasional glimpses of it can only hint at the issues submerged deeply below. For example, the female president of the 20,000-member New Jersey State Bar Association told that state's 1996 Governor's Conference on Women that "some of your biggest enemies, if you're moving up, are women."[15] Her comment struck a jarring but probably useful note of realism among hundreds of female lawyers and aspiring politicians who already knew that she was right.

There do not appear to be many female politicians who perceive support for other women as a means of *anchoring* their security—only of weakening it. In the course of my interviews, I also came across active scorn for other women, or at least an apparent preference to steer clear of them. One officeholder in her sixties expressed strong disapproval of younger female candidates with children, telling me pointedly that she never called attention to her children in the way that they do. I am reminded of one legislator who turned down my request for an interview, communicating through an aide that "she doesn't get involved with this 'woman stuff.'" I wondered to myself: with what magic does she think she can separate herself from the collective image and prospects of other women? As retired U.S. Representative Patricia Schroeder warned the new women entering Congress in 1997: "Remember that you are a voice for women—like it or not."[16]

Another representative of the group I call "the anti-women women" explained to me in great detail how she functions on a governing body that is 95% men. Essentially, her code of behavior boils down to a roster of "nevers" and "don'ts." Never identify yourself with "women's issues." Don't get too friendly with female staff. Don't admit you need to leave a meeting because of your kids (say you have an appointment). Never wear short skirts or a frilly blouse. Don't "overreact" to sexist comments. And so on. Terri Apter, who interviewed many women executives for her book *Working Women Don't Have Wives*, found some who used a similar approach. Of one such executive, Apter wrote:

> Here she was saying that her work environment was not sexist, and at the same time she was saying that in order to make it non-sexist a woman had to be very careful about what she did, how she spoke, lest she appear as a woman. There is a sharp contradiction between believing that one will not be discriminated against because one is a woman and taking such pains not to draw attention to the fact that one is a woman. If one has to non-womanize oneself to be a person, then surely one at least believes one is living in discriminatory circumstances.[17]

To use Jo Ann Boscia's phrase, this go-it-alone ethos among women does indeed seem sad—because those who did experience solidarity among women felt so emboldened. For example, many of the legislators who were part of a women's caucus (typically a bipartisan group of female lawmakers who work together on issues of shared concern) described how good it felt to set partisanship aside and focus, cooperatively and unabashedly, on matters that affect their health, opportunities, and rights *as women*. "It's the only place where I know my personal concerns will never be marginalized," commented one state senator. As Maryland's Delegate Cheryl Kagan pointed out, the feeling of comradeship can play an important role in informal settings, too:

> When there is solidarity among women legislators, it can be a tremendous source of moral support. When a group of us were defeated on a bill we really cared about, we went out together to commiserate and share war stories. It really helped us to recharge each other's batteries. Unfortunately, there just isn't as much mentoring or other support among women as there could be and should be.

Even on a local level, female officials from different communities sometimes extend a helping hand to one another. Councilwoman Judy Ferguson Shaw survived a tough recall challenge in Berkeley, Missouri, but she knows it would have been even harder without the moral support offered by female peers—even, in her case, by an officeholder hundreds of miles away in Philadelphia. "Their support really meant a lot to me, because they were the only ones who could really understand what I was going through," she remembers gratefully.

The good news is that there are women who are determined to bring something positive out of personal experiences that were negative, or at least lacking. When Mayor Joyce Savocchio first ran for office in Erie, Pennsylvania, she invited 14 representatives of women's organizations to meet with her; only 1 showed up. Nevertheless, Savocchio continues to reach out to women, especially by speaking to youth groups and encouraging young girls to consider public service careers.

Councilwoman Adele Smith of Ogden, Utah readily admits that when she decided to run, "I had no idea what I was getting myself into." Despite the unstinting support she received from women in her local chamber of commerce, Smith, a political novice, found her first race so traumatic that she came close to quitting. Even now, she feels keenly her lack of a mentor in the political arena: "I was so dumb I didn't even know I needed that kind of help," she says ruefully. "But now I understand that it's absolutely necessary, and I go out of my way to identify women who can benefit from my experience." She gave me an example:

> When I recently met a woman at a party who was running for council in a nearby city, I made a point of getting to know her. I told her everything I know. I said, "You'll have moments when you'll want to quit. When that happens, just call me and I'll help you see that things do get better." That did happen, and she did call me, and I know it helped. She was top vote-getter in that election.

Several other women who had never had a mentor also stressed that they were looking out for those who will follow them. Had a mentor been there for her, reflected Colorado Springs Councilwoman Lisa Are, "it would have taken some of the pressure off. . . .

I might have felt less alone." She was determined, though, that she'd be there for an African-American woman whom she backed to fill a vacancy on the governing body—in the face of strong efforts to seat "another white male." In Cherry Hill, New Jersey, Mayor Susan Bass Levin went so far as to set up a formal mentoring program through her office. "I think you learn quicker and better if you have a mentor, and I always wished that I'd had one. I spend a lot of time with the young people who come through our mentoring program at Town Hall, and I know it gives them personal feedback and guidance they couldn't get in any other way."

Similarly, a few who had come into contact with "queen bees" expressed a determination to suppress any such tendencies in themselves. "I'm part of the group of women who got elected in the earlier years," comments Mayor Karen Anderson of Minnetonka, Minnesota, who won her first office in 1986. "I've seen women of my generation purposely undercut the younger ones, and I think it's terrible. So I make a conscious effort to guard against that kind of behavior myself." A state senator shook her head emphatically as she said, "I'm determined to give new women in politics a helping hand—not a kick in the teeth, like a few important women gave me."

But I was especially struck by the bittersweet perspective of Pennsylvania's Commissioner Martynick. Informed, no doubt, by the wisdom of her own difficult experience, she expressed a unique blend of commitment and compassion: "I believe I have a responsibility to help other women. Sometimes, though, I feel guilty bringing more women into a business that's so very tough for them."

"Like One of the Boys"

What issues or pressures drive some women in politics to deliberately sabotage others? For obvious reasons, it was difficult to sort these out: few of my interviewees were willing to elaborate on their own disdainful comments or able to shed light on the behavior of others.

That said, there were enough common threads to stitch together at least a partial pattern. One such thread weaves through this story, related to me by a veteran city councilwoman in the Midwest:

> I'm very active in a national association of female elected and appointed officials. Recently, a young woman came to me and asked for my support in her bid to become an officer of this association. I asked what was most important to her in her work as a public official, and she told me she was primarily concerned with infrastructure problems, like roads and sewers. Well, I refused to support her. What I wanted to hear was how infrastructure issues relate to women—for example, how higher utility rates are especially devastating to poor single mothers. She couldn't address anything like that. It's not a reflection on how she does her job on her own council. She's probably very competent—but she's just like one of the boys.

Trying to satisfy others' (often conflicting) expectations of how a woman politician "should" act is seldom easy—or entirely successful. It's much like squeezing into a shoe that can be worn but never really fits. For instance, there are officeholders who express their female identities in outlook, appearance, and personality but choose to focus on exactly the same issues their male colleagues do. There is clearly nothing wrong with this, but they can be very defensive about it—because they know that voters (and colleagues) often expect something more (or different) from them. Others don't share the men's policy agendas but adopt them anyway based on routine advice that it's the only way to get ahead. Both scenarios beg the same question: How much have women won if they are still afraid to be themselves?

The same tension complicates relationships between political women. Women who have felt the sting of discrimination don't soon forget it. Like a welt, it raises their expectations of other women—and makes them unusually sensitive to perceptions of betrayal. For example, one county official took another to task for opposing a four-day work week for public employees. "I know why she did it—she's building up chits with the guys. Sure, it might help her get something she wants in the future. But she's selling out working mothers—no woman in office should ever stoop to that." Houston City Councilwoman Martha Wong has arrived at this conclusion: "We have to support other women—but only the ones who won't abandon us. And some do."

Even the vocabulary of resentment is laced with gender conflict. To describe women who gained entry into the "old boys' network" in their communities, several officeholders used the same accusatory phrase: "She got in by acting like a man." Some state lawmakers complained that the few women who had attained leadership positions in their legislatures had done so only by "doing whatever the guys told them to." Such comments touch a raw nerve in women who see themselves as simply playing the game. Others fervently believe that women, so long excluded from the playing field, should now expend some of their hard-won political capital to change the rules. This tension will not be resolved until there are enough of both types of women to achieve some sort of balance between them.

Councilwoman Pamela O'Connor of Santa Monica, California knows first-hand how painful such divisions can be. When she ran in 1994, she competed with another woman for the endorsement of a women's civic association; ironically, the group had been formed expressly to promote leadership among women. There were three contested at-large city council seats, and the other candidates were all male. Nevertheless, "some of the leaders of the group, who knew the other woman better than me, just saw me as a threat to her. So to undermine my candidacy, they called me 'the man's candidate.'" To O'Connor, who is active with the National Women's Political Caucus, such an epithet just seemed bizarre. But I heard similar ones used around the country, as women struggle to find answers for a whole new set of questions. Choosing between two women, in particular, is a political decision still freighted with symbolic dimensions that play no part in a choice between men.

Another manifestation of divisiveness among women is the weakening of some legislative women's caucuses. Indiana State Representative Mary Kay Budak was one of those who spoke with real angst on this topic: "Women used to be willing to challenge the leadership on women's issues. They often aren't anymore, and there's a real loss of camaraderie, friendship, community." She was not alone in her dismay; several legislators in different states commented that their caucuses or informal women's groups had been undermined by increasing partisanship and a sense of heightened competition.

The competition, of course, is real; the phenomenon of women running against other women is no longer unusual at any level of politics. Among many female officeholders, there is a strong perception that they are at particular risk of being challenged by women in the opposing party. This perception first struck me in a conversation with Virginia State Delegate Shirley Cooper, a veteran political warrior who has beaten every opponent in 15 years. In the middle of recounting her electoral successes, she stopped. "The only time it got close was when they ran a young woman," she admitted with a smile. "That race really gave me a scare."

"What women worry about most is that another good woman will run against them," said Jo Ann Boscia. "It's such a basic fear that it stops us from reaching out even to share information or to work on nonpartisan issues." It is not an idle fear, either: of the 10 women candidates for lieutenant governor around the country in 1996, 8 of them were running against each other![18] In part, such contests are more frequent because some women candidates are recruited solely for their chromosomes. Often, there is a cynical assumption that only females can run against (or discredit) other females—what one commentator called the "it takes a woman to trash a woman" strategy.[19]

Women also dread "catfights." There are plenty of emotional and rancorous confrontations between male politicians, too. But, said one lawmaker, "we're the ones who get labelled undignified, out of control, shrill." Visibly cringing as she recalled such an incident on the floor of her legislature, she added, "catfights reinforce those Victorian stereotypes of 'hysterical women' and make us all look bad."

One of the more widely publicized catfights in political history was New York's U. S. Senate primary in September 1992, pitting two of America's most experienced and respected female politicians against each other—former Democratic vice-presidential nominee Geraldine Ferraro vs. former U. S. Representative Elizabeth Holtzman. The bitterness of the match, particularly of Holtzman's personal attacks on Ferraro, was decried by women's advocates around the country. Ultimately, both Ferraro and Holtzman lost to Robert Abrams, and political women everywhere were confronted once again with agonizing contradictions.

Holtzman insisted that her behavior was no different from any man's. It was sexist, she pointed out, to hold female candidates to a different campaign standard. But her defense fell largely on deaf ears. In a post-election interview, prominent New York feminist Joan Hamburg responded sharply: "We didn't expect her to fight like a man—that's not the way we want women to act in the political arena."[20] Syndicated columnist Ellen Goodman called Holtzman a spoiler, arguing that if women make no effort to raise the standards of campaigning, they will accomplish nothing more than becoming "partners in a political system that's in full, cynical collapse."[21] To *Washington Post* columnist Colman McCarthy, it was a sorry spectacle of "women politicians . . . ensnared by an electoral ritual that was designed by competition-driven men. . . . They embraced the male rules of competition and abandoned sisterliness that would have enhanced their lives, in politics or out."[22] Concerned for the future, former congresswoman Bella Abzug warned: "If we adopt the worst elements of politics and make them ours, too, then it's pretty hard to make the point that women can change politics."[23]

But this same fault line was exposed again four years later. In September 1996, New York's feminist establishment wrung its hands a second time over one strong woman's challenge to another. When former State Senator Karen Burstein mounted a Democratic primary against incumbent Surrogate Court Judge Renee Roth, she, too, faced the wrath of leading women's advocates. *New York Times* columnist Joyce Purnick characterized the race as "something of a morality play for feminists," pointing out that it would have gotten little attention if judge and challenger were male.[24]

Nonetheless, influential figures like *Ms.* magazine founder Gloria Steinem insisted that the rebuke to Burstein was justified. "The point is, where do we put our slender resources in order to work toward equal representation, and one place not to put them is one good woman running against another. . . . [Things will be different] when we have 50 percent of all elected positions. But at the moment, we have to strategize together, and in this particular instance, that didn't happen."[25]

It is a point lost on none of the women I interviewed. But it leaves them with a riddle: they mustn't act like men, while they get criticized for acting like women. So what's a female politician to do?

"Women need to realize that we can't please everybody," says Sandra Miller. "We need to give ourselves—and each other—a break before anyone else will."

Fundraising Revisited: Are Women Writing the Checks?

Fundraising is the bane of political candidates, regardless of gender. On any level of politics, it is time-consuming and anxiety-provoking; those who must raise hundreds of thousands of dollars to run for the most competitive offices often find it downright degrading.

The women I interviewed had raised amounts of money ranging from a low of about $1,000 for a town council race to the $500,000 war chest accumulated by Indiana Representative Vaneta Becker in her unsuccessful bid for mayor of the city of Evansville. Almost every one perceived the amount she had to raise as "too much." There were a handful of women who termed their fundraising efforts "easy"—but most of them had been professional fundraisers!

The spiraling cost of political participation is rooted in systemic characteristics beyond the scope of this book. However, one issue that surfaced is clearly of particular concern to women: to what degree can they count on financial contributions from other women?

The answer to this question is office-dependent. Unlike female candidates for local offices, those who run for federal or statewide offices can usually count on significant support from the array of nonpartisan and/or party-affiliated women's PACs discussed earlier. Between 1990 and 1992, most of these PACs enjoyed dramatic growth; contributions to EMILY's List, for example, more than tripled.[26] It was partly due to this phenomenon that female candidates during the Year of the Woman raised unprecedented sums. One study that looked specifically at women running for open congressional seats in 1992 found that they raised, in the aggregate, $112,000 more than comparable men.[27]

There is a catch, however. Political scientist Rebekah Herrick found that such aggregate comparisons (of all female candidates in a particular type of race vs. all male candidates in the same type of race) can substantially overstate women's competitiveness. When Herrick compared individual female candidates to their male opponents *in the same contest,* she found that the women actually fell behind by an average of $129,000. Moreover, she discovered that men who ran against women in 1992 not only raised more money than women—they outraised other men, too! Puzzling over possible explanations of this phenomenon, Herrick wrote: "There could be a conspiracy to prevent women from entering the House by helping women's opponents, but this seems unlikely. Another possibility is that men candidates have more personal resources available for funding. However, this leaves open the question of why only men facing women and not men in general have more money than women candidates. A final reason is that men candidates are preferred by voters who donate money but not by other voters."[28]

Are voters who donate money somehow different from other voters? In the absence of detailed information about who gives money to various types of campaigns and why, this question is impossible to answer comprehensively. But a quick look at fundraising by female legislative candidates suggests that donors have one definitive characteristic: the vast majority are men.

This shows up plainly in some simple comparisons. Because the cost of running for a legislative seat varies enormously, I looked at four states that represent a broad range of such costs: from New Jersey, which has some of the most expensive contests in the country, to Vermont, home to some of the cheapest. Virginia and Kentucky fall in between. From each state's election commission, I obtained campaign contribution reports for five randomly selected women candidates who ran during 1994-1995. In New Jersey, these reports contain the name of every individual contributor of more than $200; in the other states, the disclosure threshold is $100.

My findings, summarized in the table below, were remarkably consistent across states, parties, and candidates. Men's names appeared on these lists more than three times as often as women's.

There is nothing inherently wrong with this pattern; in fact, it can be interpreted as proof that women are seen as viable candidates by both sexes. But it also shows that women candidates, at least on the state level, have not yet succeeded in motivating large numbers of other women to write substantial checks for them.

Does this matter, as long as female candidates are raising sufficient money from other sources? It matters to those who believe that

Table 3.1. Contributions to Female Legislative Candidates by Gender (1994-1995)

State	Avg. $ Raised by Female Candidates	Avg. # of Male Contributors*	Avg. # of Female Contributors*
New Jersey	120,591	17	4
Virginia	54,136	29	9
Vermont	6,906	4	1
Kentucky	24,390	25	7

*Reportable contributions are those over $200 in New Jersey, over $100 in other states cited.

women can and should provide the competitive edge for other women, by recruiting each other, mentoring each other, and boosting each other into office. Of course, there are other ways to demonstrate support: candidates with few female contributors may have had many female campaign volunteers, for example. But we will know that women's priorities have truly shifted when those who think nothing of spending $100 on a skirt or scarf choose instead to invest it in the political future of another woman.

Politicians with PMS

Most politically underrepresented groups in America are fiercely loyal to their own candidates. It is not unusual for African-American candidates to command over 90% of the black vote when they run against white opponents; homosexuals can depend on gays in the electorate; and so on.

Women are different. In both major parties, female voters regularly defect from females' campaigns. Two 1993 gubernatorial bids are emblematic of the problem. Mary Sue Terry, Democrat of Virginia, led George Allen among women, but too narrowly to beat him—despite many voters' perceptions from the start that he was unsupportive of issues important to women.[29] While Republican Christine Todd Whitman won New Jersey's governorship, she trailed Jim Florio among women until the very end of the campaign; even GOP women told pollsters they preferred him by as much as 28 percentage points.[30] Even during 1992, the Year of the Woman, homemakers expressed hostility toward Geraldine Ferraro's U. S. Senate candidacy, apparently seeing in it a repudiation of their own, more traditional lifestyle choices.[31] In 1990, a survey of 7000 women commissioned by *McCall's* magazine found that 35% preferred voting for a woman—but 25% would rather vote for a man.[32]

Journalist Sherrye Henry, an unsuccessful candidate for the New York State Senate in 1990, commissioned a nationwide study of the attitudes of 700 female voters toward female candidates. Her finding: 69% of respondents said that a candidate's sex made no difference to them. Significant subgroups expressed strong disapproval of women politicians, suggesting that they "suffer from PMS." As Henry wrote:

> Imagine an African-American saying the race of a candidate
> made no difference, or a gay voter saying that a homosexual
> candidate would not understand the homophobia rampant in
> society better than a heterosexual would. Obviously, you
> should examine a candidate's stand on the issues, but female
> candidates seem to lose out in all cases unless they are specif-
> ically and staunchly supported by other women. No one
> makes assumptions in their favor—and women should,
> because as a group they have the best track record by far for
> accomplishing the goals that women say are most important to
> them.[33]

There is another implication. All politicians, men and women, are most attentive to groups who support them; it is only natural to underrate the importance of those who do not. If women cannot rely on other women in the voting booth, perhaps it should come as no surprise when they do not look to each other as mentors or as anchors in the roiling waters of daily political life.

But another of Henry's findings suggests a way of bolstering the support of women for women. When respondents were told that the women in the U. S. Congress were almost entirely responsible for improving child care, funding breast cancer research, and cracking down on fathers delinquent in paying child support, their attitudes underwent a sea change. Suspicion and hostility were washed away by approval and pride.

Likewise, if women knew what motivates other women to run and to serve, they might better understand that females in office are not just politicians with PMS. Even among female officeholders, such knowledge can only strengthen mutual understanding and collegial ties.

The next chapter looks at these motivations.

4
Doing Good or Doing Favors: Motivations and Frustrations in Political Life

> *He drew a circle which shut me out,*
> *Heretic, rebel, a thing to flout;*
> *But you and I had the wit to win,*
> *We drew a circle which took him in.*
>
> —Edwin Markham

Maureen: Preserving a Personal Identity

"For years after I was elected to political office, I kept denying that I was a politician," chuckles Maureen. She has spent a decade in the state senate and now serves as chair of its powerful Joint Appropriations Committee. But even her current status as one of the three or four most influential women in her state has not changed Maureen's outlook.

"I still think of politicians as people who have no identity, no life outside of the political arena," she explains. "I've never been that way. My title is very important and it enables me to do a lot of good, so naturally it's a source of satisfaction. But Maureen the person—the mom, the spouse, the professional—will always be separate from Maureen the senator."

She got into politics by accident. Outgoing and gregarious by nature, the former teacher and businesswoman entered partisan politics by way of social contacts and community groups. She became a party enthusiast, a volunteer, and then, when her children were older, a full-time staffer. When another female legislator unexpectedly resigned her seat, Maureen was appointed to fill the vacancy.

"Because I was filling an unexpired term, I was able to learn the job before I had to run for it. That made all the difference....I don't think I ever would have run otherwise. I was terrified of it!"

Observing her now, one would never guess at that early terror. She is strong in her convictions, outspoken, and self-confident. Surrounded by the trappings of power—luxurious office, large and deferential staff, a constant stream of visitors vying for her attention—she is the very picture of political success.

But Maureen never loses sight of the serendipitous nature of that success. "I never planned this, and I had built a rich, rewarding life long before I entered the legislature. That's why I know I'll have one again when I leave." Indeed, she already thinks in terms of life beyond the statehouse; though at the top of her political game, she is seriously considering an opportunity to return to the private sector. Both financially and personally, it makes sense to her—which a protracted sojourn in full-time political life does not.

Maureen is certain that such a move would be incomprehensible to most of her male colleagues—who, she believes, cannot imagine a satisfying existence without the prestige and power of their offices. "Their self-esteem—their whole identity—gets completely wrapped up in the office they hold. They're the ones who insist on being addressed as 'Mr. Senator' for years after they've retired or lost their seats."

Recounting her many legislative accomplishments over the years, Maureen takes enormous pride in having made a difference for the citizens of her state. She glows when she describes her hard-won committee chairmanship. If she continues a full-time legislative career, she will probably seek another leadership post. But that is neither her only option, nor necessarily the most attractive one.

"I've done everything I set out to do in this office, and then some," she observes contentedly. "I'm very grateful to have had such opportunities. But when I'm ready, it won't be hard at all to let go—and I won't expect to be called 'Senator' any more, only 'Grandma!' "

A Career—Or a Calling?

The motivations and orientation of most women I talked to run counter to a pervasive norm in modern political life. Careerism—officeholding planned as a lifelong, self-defining career—is simply alien to Maureen and others like her. Typically, they entered politics circuitously and unexpectedly. Having already raised children, held a job, or done both together or sequentially, they have little interest in another long-term occupation for its own sake—but rather for what it allows them to accomplish. Connecticut State Representative Claudia Powers, herself a former educator and mother of four, puts it this way: "Women do a lot of different things in their lives—they usually decide to tackle politics after they've spent time being wives, mothers, and workers. The difference is that men in politics tend to be much more single-minded and unidirectional about it."

One of Maryland's most senior female legislators, State Senator Barbara Hoffman has watched many new women and men move up in politics during the last decade. In her experience, a careerist orientation develops early—and tends to appear among young men:

> When I was spending a lot of time in our state party office, we often got young men coming in to volunteer. When I asked them about their career plans, a lot of them would say, "I want to be a politician." And I would tell them that there's no such thing—there's no job description for a "politician." You have to make something of yourself, I think, before you have anything to offer the voters.

A nationwide survey of more than 1200 female candidates found that the overwhelming majority wished to serve in elective office for 12 years or less. Among candidates for state legislatures, only one in five indicated a desire to serve "more than 12 years and make a career of officeholding." The study's author, political scientist Susan Carroll, also noted that "sizable minorities of candidates expressed a desire to serve only for four or fewer years."[1]

Conducted in the late 1970's, this survey is quite dated. However, I found little evidence that women's attitudes have changed. One of the more clear-cut examples is Richmond City Councilwoman Viola Baskerville. Even before she completed her first term, she made a point of telling the regional magazine *Northside:* "I don't look at it as a career. Six years is the maximum for a locally elected official. After that, they become less effective as leaders."[2] To New York Assemblywoman Susan John, overly long tenures signal diminishing initiative:

> People figure out that the less you do in the legislature, the fewer enemies you make and the longer you can stay. I hate

to say it, but with a few exceptions, I've observed that legislators who are here for 20 or 30 years get like that. To do this job right, I think you should make a commitment for a limited period, focus on it intensely during that period—and then get out of the way.

Maryland's Delegate Cheryl Kagan has noticed that her male colleagues commonly have what she calls "10 Year Plans" for their political advancement but that the women in the legislature almost never do. To Senator Hoffman, this difference flows naturally from the unplanned nature of many women's political involvement. "Because most of us get into politics by accident, we don't view it as a career, like many men do. Women don't internalize it as much. That's important because it means that we can walk away from all the pomp and circumstance when we choose to, without a backward glance."

Interestingly, Hoffman's comments were echoed by the youngest officeholder I interviewed. Town Meeting Representative Stephanie Hunter Sanchez of Greenwich, Connecticut is under 30—arguably someone who should perceive fewer differences between women and men in politics than the generation who preceded her. But she, too, observed that "men are much more conditioned to see politics as a long-term career option. In fact, I don't know a single other woman in my age group who views it that way."

A recent study reported that women elected officials are as likely as men to say that they will run for another term or that they aspire to the nation's highest offices.[3] It is not necessarily a contradiction to add, as over half of my interviewees did, that their ambitions and aspirations have strings attached. One intends to run for higher office if she can work out her child care problems; another will seek a third term if a private-sector opportunity does not pan out; many voiced the conviction that "when it isn't fun anymore, I intend to get out." Rarely did I hear anything to contradict the observation of Christina Selin, councilwoman in New Rochelle, New York: "The women I know in politics do it because they enjoy it. Career politicians, women or men, are different; what's paramount to them is saving the job, saving the income."

If unalloyed careerism is indeed unusual among female elected officials, this is striking because there are often strong incentives to stay in office as long as possible. One such incentive is the public pension system, open to legislators in all but eight states and sometimes to local officials as well. Its benefits are usually tied to length of service, thus encouraging a careerist approach. For example, in New York, New Jersey, Nevada, Hawaii, Arizona, and Connecticut, a lawmaker must serve for at least 10 years to become eligible for a pension. Longer tenures enable legislators in some states to begin drawing their benefits at age 55 or younger.[4]

While no one gets rich in public service, pensions (along with health insurance, which is often provided as well) are not trivial rewards—particularly for part-time legislators maintaining outside employment that provides its own benefits. A few examples: a 20-year lawmaker can retire with over $4800 per month in Indiana, $2840 in Texas, and $2133 in Oklahoma.[5] How many part-time jobs in the private sector can compare?

It is true that legislators' salaries can be absurdly low given the importance of their work—some earn no more than $5 or $10 a day. But experts have identified a recent pattern of steadily increasing legislative salaries in many states.[6] (There is also an important philosophical issue: what is the meaning of public "service" if citizen legislatures are expected to compete with the private sector in pay and perquisites? Is elective officeholding just another job?) Be that as it may, there are surely some politicians who extend their terms in office simply to build up a nest egg.

There is absolutely no evidence to suggest that women officeholders are uninterested in financial compensation—or that men are unduly influenced by it. But there is certainly some tension around these issues. When I asked about the factors that influenced their political career plans, several women instantly shot back: "Well, I'm not one of those guys who sticks around forever just to buck up his pension!" Not only did these comments sound unusually brittle, but they stood out as non sequiturs, since I had never *asked* about pensions.

Perhaps unwittingly, the idea that women legislators are less focused on financial rewards than men came up in a 1996 debate in the Massachusetts statehouse. Arguing against a proposed pay cut for legislators, Representative Jim Fagan made a prediction: "Should this (pay cut) be allowed to happen, we will have a government of boys, housewives and the idiot children of the idle rich."[7] One wonders how his "housewife" colleagues reacted to this remark.

The Politics of Power

Whatever the appeal of money, it is clearly augmented by the lure of power. Many of the women I interviewed expressed some ambivalence about power. A few seemed indifferent to it. But almost all believed that women officeholders perceive, value, and wield power differently than men.

Ambivalence about power was most frequently expressed by women who spent years as community volunteers or grassroots activists before running for office. They had cut their teeth on policy, not politics; long service with nonpartisan issue-based organizations like the League of Women Voters had honed their skills in analysis and persuasion but not necessarily in how to build or exercise political power. To be successful politicians, they needed to learn such skills. And they did—but not without a measure of discomfort or, sometimes, distaste. The mayor of a small Midwestern city described her conflicting feelings this way:

> I think of power as my ability to get things done. Because of my position, important people return my phone calls and municipal employees rush to do what I tell them. That's flattering and gratifying—I can't say I don't like it. But I'm very uncomfortable with special favors, like getting my street cleaned before any of the others in my neighborhood. And I hate to feel that I'm getting my way on an issue not because I'm right, but because I'm the mayor. That's power—but it's not why I wanted this job.

One of the few women who seemed completely comfortable with the notion of power was Karen Anderson, mayor of Minnetonka, Minnesota, who offered enthusiastically (and without being asked): "Oh, I enjoy the power of being mayor!" But Anderson also believes that many people would be "shocked," as she put it, to hear her talk openly about how much she enjoys being powerful. "I'm a little embarrassed to talk about it," she admitted. "I think a lot of women see power as self-serving. But what's important is how you use it; it shouldn't be for your own financial or career benefit. Too many others have used it that way—I believe that I use it for the good of my community."

More of the officeholders had a visceral—and highly negative—reaction to my question about what it meant to them to have power.

At the very mention of it, Virginia legislator Shirley Cooper bristled. Revealing much about what she has observed—and resented—during more than a decade in the House of Delegates, she told me: "I'm not here to make my law firm bigger. That's what makes most women different. We're not out grabbing each other by the neck and fighting for power." She went further, suggesting that women who seek power like men do are punished by the electorate: "There have been a few women elected who were motivated by the power. But they don't last. They may get in, but then they get voted out."

Others equated power with egotism and self-aggrandizement and took pains to disassociate themselves from such characteristics. Maryland's Montgomery County Councilwoman Betty Ann Krahnke drew this distinction: "People run either to be somebody, or to do something. I'm in the second category." Indiana Representative Vaneta Becker shook her head disapprovingly as she talked about "the kind of power I don't want, power for the sake of being able to control people." When Judy Knudson served as chair of the Board of Supervisors in Virginia's James City County, she wielded no small degree of influence herself; nonetheless, she observed flatly, "I look at power and I think 'arrogant.' "

Councilwoman Adele Smith of Ogden, Utah agonized over the corrupting influence of power. It was a dimension that others hinted at but seemed too uncomfortable to discuss. "In a sense, the power is frightening to me," she reflected. "I'd be afraid to have too much power because I don't want to change. I want to be the same person I was before I got elected." What kind of change did she fear? "I don't want to be pushing people around and making them resent me," she added. The subtext is clear: power makes people do things and behave in ways that are unnatural, even repugnant. If this is one's conception of power, it must surely take time (not to mention psychological struggle) to feel good about amassing it.

As a marketing researcher, I always kept in mind the fact that people are often less than candid when asked about behaviors or attitudes that might put them in an unfavorable light. For example, a socially desirable behavior like voting is usually overreported by about 25% in personal interviews; conversely, a potentially embarrassing behavior—such as reading pulp magazines—may be understated by as much as 50%.

When discussing power, I was sensitive to this kind of bias. Perhaps women were unwilling to admit that they avidly sought power and exercised it much as men do. They might think that I—or more importantly, their constituents who read this book—would disapprove.

So in this instance, I looked for actions that would corroborate what the women told me. Without much difficulty, I found them. Virginia State Senator L. Louise Lucas unhesitatingly declined the opportunity to seek a legislative leadership post, which packs a wallop in political muscle and prestige. Why? "That's more of an ego thing. It wouldn't amount to a hill of beans for my constituents. What matters to me is being able to produce for them....I don't ever want to have to vote a certain way or do a lot of favors for people just so I can get a leadership role in the Senate." In New York's legislature, leadership posts are enticing for another reason: they carry stipends up to $30,000 above a lawmaker's base pay of $57,500.[8] Nonetheless, such jobs didn't tempt Assemblywoman John, either: "I think there's too much of the rebel in me—or maybe not enough of the pragmatist."

Councilwoman Adele Smith of Ogden, Utah resisted a good deal of pressure to run for mayor, despite the $60,000 salary and considerable importance of her town's chief executive. Like several others on the local level, Pennsylvania's Bucks County Commissioner Sandra Miller had been approached to run for a seat in the state legislature but turned it down: "I asked them, what's the prize? Three nights a week in the capital?" For Jo Ann Boscia, council president in Lakewood, Ohio, there was an even more tempting offer: appointment to a legislative seat that would imminently become vacant. Her response: "I decided that's not what I want to do with the rest of my life."

In terms of how they experience power, these highly individualistic women have more company than they might think. Several studies suggest that "womanpower" is often distinctive in the corporate world, too.[9] For example, a global survey of female and male business leaders commissioned by the International Women's Forum found that women attributed their success to "personal power," arising from charisma, accomplishments, and contacts, while men relied on "structural power," based on position, title, and the ability to reward or punish.[10] Similar distinctions have been identified among women and men who wield power in the public sector; a study of state government administrators and political appointees in Arizona concluded that more men than women wielded "position power," anchored by organizational authority and control of resources.[11]

And at least one researcher suspects that businesswomen are seriously handicapped by the way they wield—or fail to wield—power. When Liz Roman Gallese interviewed 24 of the most senior female executives in America, she discovered that all of them felt valued for their "thinking power": the ability to solve problems, manage subordinates, and master technical expertise. But they knew they were disadvantaged at the highest echelons, the world of big deals, bare knuckles, and raw nerve. As one of the executives observed candidly: "When it's guts-balls leverage, when it's fighting, when it's playing poker, when it's 'I bet my 4 zillion dollars on this deal, where are you?' the world doesn't think women can do that. And I don't know how many women think women can do that."[12]

She could have been talking about the world of politics, too.

Why Do It?

There are probably as many individual reasons to run for office as there are races. However, research on female candidates' motivations suggests that more of them run to advance community goals than their own careers. The same appears to be true of female political activists in general: a study of 3000 women and men involved in California politics over a 22-year period found that in both parties, significantly more women than men were driven to action primarily by concern for particular issues.[13] Anita Hummer's story is typical: now mayor pro tem of Elizabeth City, North Carolina, she ran for office because rocks were thrown at her home. First she got involved in a Community Watch group and then decided that the best way to stand up against crime in her hometown was to run for city council. In Houston, Texas, Councilwoman Martha Wong got her start by protesting the construction of an athletic facility that she viewed as too big for the neighborhood. The experience of Minnetonka, Minnesota Mayor Karen Anderson was only slightly different: having rewritten her city's zoning ordinances as part of an appointed commission, she ran for office because she wanted a say in implementing the new rules. As women like these have approached it, politics is not a personal career path but a community problem-solving tool.

When one of the lead characters in the popular TV sitcom *Designing Women* decided to run for office, her motives fit this mold. It was clear to the audience that Julia Sugarbaker, a businesswoman in her forties, never planned to get involved in politics. But in an episode titled "The Candidate," she became enraged by the sexist comments of a male candidate and decided that the only way to root out gender bias was to challenge him. Apparently, the show's writers assumed that Julia's decision would be believable to her (mostly female) fans.

Political scientists Timothy Bledsoe and Mary Herring point out that women's issue orientation may also mean that "women are less likely to perceive their involvement in politics as 'professional' in terms of competitive strategies."[14] Indeed, another finding of the California study was that even as women become increasingly ambitious, they do not necessarily focus more on personal ascendancy than on issue advocacy. Richmond City Councilwoman Viola Baskerville is direct and unabashed about her ambition to become mayor of that city—an office which is not elected by the voters but appointed from among the councilmembers themselves. But she is even more determined not to "do deals," the time-honored way of currying favor among colleagues. No matter what, she insists, "I won't trade votes—I've made it very clear that I have to believe in an issue in order to support it. I won't stand with you on something just so that you'll do x-y-z for me." In the same vein, some state legislators observed that their male colleagues worked harder to develop "stables" of protégés and others beholden to them for favors, jobs, or votes. New York's Assemblywoman John noted that her male colleagues devote more effort to "the networking part of politics. The women are more focused on the substance of developing legislation."

To be sure, there are women with a keen appreciation of competitive strategies and great skill at deploying them. One such woman is Maryland's Delegate Cheryl Kagan. In the independent publication *Guide to Maryland Legislators 1995-1998*, this first-term officeholder is described as follows: "She took to lawmaking Annapolis-style like today's kids take to computer games: she didn't just know the basics, she knew and used the fanciest moves."[15] But even Kagan senses that her approach is atypical among women: "Women hold the reins of power more lightly than men," she suggests. "I think that's one of the reasons why women are willing to take risks on tough votes. Many men stay focused on reelection and rising through leadership ranks."

Political efficacy—believing that they can make a difference—is extremely important to female officeholders, particularly in the absence of careerist motivations. Maryland's Montgomery County Councilwoman Krahnke spoke for many of them: "I think a lot of women are uncomfortable with the accolades and the glory if they don't feel they're making a difference." But if they do feel they're making a difference, that sense of accomplishment can clearly keep them going even in the face of disappointments and setbacks. When Virginia Senator L. Louise Lucas and I left her office at Norfolk State University after her interview, she was stopped by a young man who wanted to tell her that she had inspired him to pursue a graduate degree. The speech she had given at his commencement exercises, he said, had changed his life. Visibly moved, Lucas turned to me: "You see? That's what keeps me going. That's what it's all about."

Some women are convinced that their presence alone is meaningful to their constituents. "I'm constantly getting calls from women in the community about problems that I can't do much about, like child support disputes or divorce proceedings," says a county commissioner. "But it seems to make them feel better just to talk to someone they can relate to in government, someone who can put a human face on 'officialdom.' And I know they call me only because I'm female—they tell me so." Commissioner Miller, too, receives such calls. A Democrat, she shares with amusement that many of the callers begin by saying, "I'm a Republican, but...."

As much as women seek to make a difference in their communities by serving in office, they sometimes recognize that the experience makes an even bigger difference in them. This, too, can be a major source of satisfaction and psychic rewards. I often heard the word "leadership": women talked about learning to exercise it, teach it, and model it for others. Interestingly, there was no one definition of leadership. To one, it meant being able to control a raucous public meeting; to another, it had to do with bringing people together. But it was always linked to pride in the officeholding role and a sense that few other life experiences offered such opportunities for personal growth. When I asked Adele Smith whether all her travails in public office were worth it, her smile lit up the room. "I was a leader all my life, but I never knew it," she answered. "Now I do...and it feels so good!"

The "Old Boys' Network"

One factor that impinges on women's political efficacy is their exclusion from informal networks or groups that they perceive as helping to advance the careers of men. I heard about the "old boys' network" in the modest offices of town councilwomen and in the palatial suites of state senators; it cropped up even where the "boys" weren't old and the governing body included a significant number of females.

Irwin Gertzog, author of *Congressional Women*, has traced the operation of these groups into the House of Representatives, though he argues that their influence has fallen off in recent years.[16] On lower levels of politics and government, the weakening of "old boys' networks—if it is occurring at all—is much less apparent. According to Maryland's Hoffman: "A lot of important decisions are made in informal settings, like at lunch or on the golf course, and women just aren't there. Even when women are attorneys and have access to that whole professional network, they're not members of the 'club.' " Georgia's Hart ticks off on her fingers: "The hunting clubs, the bars, the golf course....Those are the places where the 'old boys' get together." Despite more public scrutiny of legislative processes than ever before, some women feel that these informal groups still play a pivotal—and largely unfettered—role in shaping policy and politics.

In Elizabeth City, North Carolina, Mayor Pro Tem Anita Hummer describes how after her 1993 election, she found that "the city manager, the finance chairman, and the mayor would make decisions among themselves and then just come into council meetings and say that 'we've decided such-and-such.' Sometimes they'd carry on a meeting as though I just wasn't here; I felt like saying 'Hey, wait a minute! I'm here, too!' " As Gwenn Klingler recalls being the sole female alderman among 10 men in Springfield, Illinois during the early 1990's: "Some of them just didn't take me seriously. I had made a decision not to hang out with them at a bar after council meetings, so I was left out of a lot of the deal-making and information-sharing."

I wouldn't try telling Judy Knudson that the "old boys' network" is losing its influence. She has seen its members block the advancement of outsiders who can't or won't do things their way:

> Recently there was an opening on one of our important county boards, and the only candidate for the position was an outspoken woman who had been a thorn in the side of the local establishment. All of a sudden, they extended the deadline for candidates to come forward. And sure enough, this new candidate appeared—a guy who was active in the chamber of commerce, big lawyer in town. And guess who got appointed!

This story wouldn't surprise Mayor Alice Schlenker of Lake Oswego, Oregon. Since she mounted an unsuccessful primary challenge for a state legislative seat against a well-connected man, "neither he nor the 'old boys' around him have ever forgiven me. In the six years I've been mayor, they've never accepted me."

Several state legislators believe that the "old boys' network" is perpetuated by lobbyists—representatives of companies or institutions who often spend as much time (if not more) in statehouses as the lawmakers themselves. Their job is to influence legislation, so relationships with legislators are their stock in trade. Where do they cement these relationships? Traditionally, where women aren't. One observer of how Washington lobbyists curry favor with congressmen said bluntly: "They fish together, they hunt together, they play cards together, and they whore together."[17]

"These lobbyists are pretty powerful people, in the capitol building every day, and they can be very paternalistic—patting women on the head and so on," commented Delaware State Senator Patricia Blevins. Indiana Representative Vaneta Becker added that female legislators have to be careful about where and when they spend time with male lobbyists: "Otherwise, people will start to talk." But Becker's colleague, Representative Mary Kay Budak, isn't sure that lack of comfort and of access are the real problems: "Even when I played golf with them, they wouldn't discuss issues in depth with me. I think their attitude was, 'What does she know?' "

At the meetings of local governing bodies, there are often community business representatives who function much like state lobbyists. Female officeholders in communities both large and small told of being ignored or dismissed by these representatives (who are almost invariably male). In Detroit, Michigan, Councilwoman Maryann Mahaffey took the initiative in approaching some utility executives: "They proceeded to ignore me. It's partly because they tend to focus on the mayor, but it's also because I'm a woman." Johnson City, Tennessee is a fraction the size of Detroit, but industry representatives appear in its city hall, too. There, it is the mayor who is ignored—Mayor Mickii Carter, the only female member of the city's governing body.

When asked what advice they'd give to others about how to succeed in politics, several women answered with a rueful smile: "I'd tell them: learn to play golf!" But women's exclusion from these networks and groups is no joke. According to management consultant Michael Zey, such networks form a "shadow organization"—intangible, unseen, and unacknowledged, but often at the heart of the power structure and the source of critical information for those who wish to move up.[18] In a 1995 survey conducted by Catalyst, an independent women's research organization, 461 top corporate women cited "exclusion from informal networks of communication" as the second most important barrier to their advancement in American business. (It is interesting to note that among the male chief executives who were also included in the Catalyst study, only 15% saw this as a serious problem for women.[19] Such a significant split in perceptions is a problem in itself.)

Harvard University researcher Herminia Ibarra suggests that even when women achieve access to an influential network, their ties to it are likely to be weaker and less productive than those of men.[20] Ibarra's finding resonates in the experience of this county commissioner:

> I've served in this office, with the same group of men, for more than five years. We get along fine professionally, and I can't say that they've ever excluded me from discussions of public business. But every week after our commission meeting, they all go out to lunch together—and never, in all this time, have they invited me to join them. I know darn well that those lunches are all about political gossip and strategy, and it really undermines my political effectiveness to be out of the loop. Since we're all in the same party, there's no reason why I shouldn't be on the inside. But—intentionally or not—they've kept me out.

Some of the women I interviewed made a point of telling me that female politicians must "get smarter" about playing by conventional (male-established) rules. Until many things change, this is undoubtedly true. But some of the same women complained that the "old boys' network" obfuscates those rules. This creates a conundrum: How can women follow rules they can't figure out? Indeed, Mayor Susan Bass Levin of Cherry Hill, New Jersey describes politics as "an insider's game." She elaborates: "There are lots and lots of rules in politics, and none of them are written down. During my first couple of years I didn't even know the rules were there....All these conversations were going on around me, and I didn't know enough to pay attention." Houston City Councilwoman Martha Wong has found the rules "highly disguised." A former school principal, she falls back on her professional skills of observation and study to help her decipher what goes on: who is allied with whom, what deals have been struck, whether there is room for compromise, and so on.

When women feel they aren't privy to the rules, it can be especially frustrating when these rules seem to change arbitrarily. Indiana's Representative Budak believed that she had earned a shot at legislative leadership, only to have it whisked away:

> I remember going to the Speaker when I was first elected and saying, "I notice that you have all men in leadership, and most of them are from the same part of the state, too." He said to me, "Mary Kay, you're just a newcomer. You have to wait your turn." That didn't sound unreasonable to me. But now that I've built up a lot of seniority, it seems like the rules have changed. Now it's "the youngest and the brightest"—and I've noticed that the youngest and brightest are usually men.

Some find ways around the unofficial rules—ironically, by mastering the official ones. Knowing that their influence is limited in the "back room," they push issues of concern out front, into public view. This strategy was used successfully by a mayor who believed that commercial building approvals in her town were being quietly approved "between friends" without sufficient scrutiny of their residential impacts. Just as quietly, she helped form a neighborhood citizens' group, which began attending public meetings to ask questions about the proposed developments. This intervention slowed the approval process and opened it up to broader input. From then on, the mayor felt that her influence on land use planning was greatly magnified. In a twist on this approach, Anita Hummer started her own talk radio show in Elizabeth City, North Carolina. She found that arguments that failed to resonate with her city council colleagues were more influential with her radio audience—helping to generate public pressure behind her initiatives.

In light of their increasing, if maddeningly slow, electoral gains during the past two decades, it seems surprising that more women have not broken through these old walls. There are now some local and state governmental bodies with a critical mass, if not a majority, of female members. We would expect the climate in such institutions to reflect their new diversity.

In some ways, it surely does. Recent evidence suggests, for instance, that women legislators have greater influence with their male colleagues when state legislatures have more than a token number of female members, and that men in those legislatures are more willing to take up "women's issues."[21] But the overall dynamics may be more complicated. In a three-year study of one hundred female and male managers, researchers at the Wellesley College Center for Research on Women found a disquieting pattern: when the number of women in male-dominated organizations exceeded 15%, resistance to them actually became more overt.[22] Suddenly, the women were no longer novelties or neophytes but credible competition; benign acceptance soured into resentment. The Wellesley findings were buttressed by a later study of 1705 workers at a California state agency and two Fortune 100 firms: analysts at the University of California found that the more women there were in work units, the more men indicated a sense of detachment from the organization. (Interestingly, women had the opposite reaction: gender integration increased their feelings of commitment to the organization.[23])

In early 1997, *Business Week* featured an analysis of women's progress in major corporations during the 1990's. In line with the Wellesley and University of California research, it revealed a backlash among men in just those companies where substantial numbers of women had finally broken through to the executive suite. "The threat of a white male backlash unnerves many employers," the magazine reported, resulting in the abandonment of targeted training programs and other supports. "With women fleeing big companies in search of flexibility and control, those left will be hard-pressed to achieve the critical mass to alter their companies markedly."[24]

Only time will tell whether such patterns develop in political institutions as more and more of them pass the 15% mark, identified in the Wellesley study as a key threshold. Currently, 23 state legislatures are still less than 20% female (when both upper and lower houses are combined).[25]

Also, old expectations and modes of behavior have deep roots. Richmond, Virginia is the state's capital, a diverse city of 200,000 that exemplifies the "New South." But when Viola Baskerville first ran for city council in 1994, she found her credibility undermined by people who referred to her—an attorney and well-known civic activist—as "the doctor's wife." A more general problem, pointed out by Maryland's County Councilwoman Betty Ann Krahnke: "When a woman tries to move aggressively on an issue, she's a bitch—a man is making progress, getting action. You have to have a lot of self-confidence to get beyond that,...and your self-confidence gets battered all the time."

Other officeholders regaled me with tales of being mistaken for secretaries, embarrassed by sexual innuendoes, and belittled by nicknames like "Prettyface." Mayor Mickii Carter of Johnson City, Tennessee suffered a particularly humiliating experience after her election in 1993: "Right after I got elected, the men on my city commission took bets on how long it would take to make me cry. The former mayor bet $50 that he could do it in less than six months." Granted, such things are small and petty and rarely affect overall legislative or political effectiveness. But they can chip away at one's general comfort level, eroding the sense of belonging to an institution or group. "Sure I fit in. I do the same work and have access to the same resources as everyone else," said a city councilwoman. "But there's a lot of camaraderie here that I just don't feel part of."

The climate of a corporate or political organization has other facets, too. One of those facets is the informal, on-the-job training and feedback available to new entrants. There are apparently some political initiation processes routinely open to men but still closed to women. Connecticut State Representative Claudia Powers described one:

> Young women coming up in politics are especially vulnerable to being attacked for lack of experience, but at the same time they don't get the kind of coaching that men do. For example, I attended a campaign debate recently where the female candidate—a political newcomer in her twenties—made a really

serious mistake in one of her statements about the way government operates. Now, I know that if a man had made a mistake like that, his party leadership and his running mates would just take him out and yell at him, and he'd never do it again. But with a young woman, it's different. Nobody knew what to do with her. They just sat there in shock. She won't have the same opportunity to learn from her mistakes that a young man would.

In the same vein, I was struck by how often women wished they could get more constructive and timely feedback from better-established colleagues. Rachel, the county commissioner profiled in Chapter 2, was convinced that she would have had a better shot at a legislative nomination had party leaders told her their concerns about her family responsibilities. One legislator bemoaned how she'd "spent months on a wild goose chase, trying to get support for a bill that my senior committee members knew was doomed from the start. Why didn't they say something to me, so that I would have saved time—and saved face? I think it's because they thought I'd break down and cry!"

Similar concerns echo in the experiences of corporate women. Summarizing her series of interviews with women in middle management, business professor Rose Mary Wentling underscores this point: "Without feedback on job performance, women cannot improve their work, corrections cannot be made, and problems can escalate until they are beyond repair. One woman worked for a manager who continually refused to offer her any negative feedback. He told her she was doing a great job, but she heard differently during her annual performance review when he lashed her with criticism."[26] While men may have similar experiences, women are less likely to have mentors or informal networks to help them work through the feelings of anger and discouragement. At any rate, most would recognize Wentling's anecdote as a cautionary tale.

A "Typical Woman"

Female officeholders sense that they are easily stereotyped, both by their colleagues and by their constituents. The corollary: they must work overtime—literally—to prove that they're not just "typical women."

What is a "typical woman"? Varied though the answers were, they all boiled down to the same essence: she is simply not as competent and tough as a typical man. Commissioner Miller has been told that a typical woman is someone who shows an interest in landscaping: "People warn me not to get involved with a project to beautify the landscaping around our public buildings. They say I'll look like Lady Bird Johnson!" To another officeholder, it means someone who actively and publicly promotes other women: "You get labeled pretty fast, and you have to be careful not to look as though that's all you're interested in. It's very threatening." Lakewood, Ohio Council President Jo Ann Boscia perceives "a stereotype that women can't be tough, that we can't make hard decisions, that if we get into a crisis we'll cry."

Such notions are rooted deeply in the earth of history and conventional imagery: men are supposed to make hard, impersonal (especially financial) decisions in the public sphere, leaving women free to be soft, sentimental, and emotionally expressive nurturers at home. Indeed, as recently as 1991, nearly one in five Americans (19%) told pollsters that "women should run their homes and children and leave running the country to men." Close to one in three (27%) agreed with the statement that "most men are better suited emotionally for politics." Why are there so few women at the top of the political ladder? Respondents to the 1989 Virginia Slims Poll believed one of the most important reasons was that "most Americans aren't ready to elect a woman to higher office."[27]

Women have enjoyed the most electoral success at the local level, in part because hometown government smacks of family and community—not big-time, tough-guy political brawls. Indeed, traditional biases are alive and well at town hall. At least a third of voters surveyed in Cincinnati, Ohio believed that male city council candidates would make stronger leaders and decision-makers than women. Who would perform better in a crisis? Though female voters saw no gender difference, male voters overwhelmingly put their trust in other men.[28]

Stereotypes snake into many corners of political life. When Miller was first elected, county staff immediately presented her with reports about children and youth services. "It was my first day on the job, and immediately they wanted to pigeonhole me! Of course I care about those issues, but my interests are much broader than that." New Rochelle, New York Councilwoman Selin held a fashion show fundraiser for her campaign: "I was so surprised to hear the comment 'It's nice you feel you could do something like that as a woman.' The implication is that it's somehow risky to do 'feminine' things." Illinois Representative Gwenn Klingler consciously guards her demeanor on the floor of the legislature: "Otherwise, they'll say you're just an 'emotional woman.'"

Like burrs, stereotypes can attach themselves to the most unlikely victims. Maryland State Delegate Cheryl Kagan, a single professional woman and accomplished politician in her mid-thirties, certainly fits no traditional feminine image. And yet, she found herself the unwitting—and unhappy—subject of tongue-in-cheek newspaper articles all over the country with titles like "All for the Love of a Legislator" and "Wining, Dining and Wooing—The Ethics of Courtship." What set off the explosive press attention? Kagan simply followed a state law that required her to disclose all gifts she had accepted from lobbyists. Because the man she is dating is a lobbyist, she dutifully listed his various expenditures on gifts to her, entertainment, and trips they had taken together. The total—about $2000—made her the Maryland legislature's number 1 gift-getter and brought down an avalanche of attention on her personal life.

But what irks Kagan is that two of her colleagues, who were romantically involved with female lobbyists, completely escaped criticism for failing to report equivalent expenditures. Says Kagan indignantly, "In the context of a modern relationship, it's impossible to believe that the women never bought a bottle of wine, paid for theatre tickets, picked up the restaurant check, whatever. But society's assumption is still that 'boy pays, boy buys.' So nobody questioned the fact that they disclosed nothing." Adding wearily that even *Glamour* magazine had expressed an interest in her story—for their Valentine's Day issue—Kagan concluded, "The thing is, I'm really tired of being a girlfriend. I just want to be a legislator again."

Evidence suggests that male legislators believe voters see their female colleagues as mainly interested in "women's issues." This is the finding of a 1988 study of perceptions of women in four state legislatures, which also showed that men share very similar views about the factors that make women electable—which women do not. Extrapolating from their data, the study's authors mused: "Perhaps this assumption, that women in the legislatures are very similar to each other, means that other assumptions are also held, such as all women vote a certain way or women will serve best on certain types of committees."[29]

Of course, there are positive stereotypes, too, partly perpetuated by women themselves. For example, the same 1988 study found that a much higher percentage of female than male legislators believed that women in politics bring about better government. Many of those I interviewed described women politicians as more "caring" or "sensitive" than men. Voters characterize female candidates as more likely than male candidates to be honest, moral, upright, and understanding of people's needs.[30] A 1990 survey found that majorities of both women and men believe female elected officials are better at dealing with the problems of families and working parents.[31]

Such positive attributions notwithstanding, women often seem baffled by preconceived notions about how they should think, react, or behave. Here is a councilwoman's self-described "pet peeve":

> I hate when people bring babies and little children to public hearings to make some point about a public health or safety matter. They seem to think that because I'm a mother, the crying kids influence me more than grownup arguments do. I once had an angry constituent yell at me that as a mother, I should be ashamed of a decision I'd made. Regardless of the merits of my vote, I never heard anybody attack the men on the council for being bad fathers!

In 1984, *Boston Globe* columnist Ellen Goodman poked fun at some of these stereotypes. Reminding her readers that traditional expectations can linger subconsciously even when voters claim to reject them, she noted one political consultant's fantasy of a TV commercial for the perfect female candidate:

> In one 60-second spot, she lands a multimillion-dollar jet plane in an ice storm while caring for the male copilot who has suddenly become ill. She then makes a brilliant presentation on a deal that involves millions, and whips the cash out of her briefcase while her name flashes across the screen. Decisive, caring, organized and able to deal with big budgets–the best of both sexes–she wins the election.[32]

Looking toward the future, Goodman was hopeful that the electorate would begin to jettison some of this baggage. Until then, she concluded, women would "have to keep flying airplanes through the ice storms."

Unfortunately, many remain in the air.

Structural Problems

One of the biggest frustrations in political life has little to do with gender. For both women and men, especially at higher levels of office, there are simply very few opportunities to move up because of the power of incumbency. For better or worse, incumbent officeholders attract the lion's share of money, name recognition, and credibility in the vast majority of races.

Running against an incumbent is no harder for an individual female candidate than for a male candidate, assuming roughly equal qualifications. Collectively, however, women are disadvantaged because most incumbents are still men. All but 2 of the 24 women newly elected to the U. S. House of Representatives in 1992 won in races where the seat was open—in other words, they faced no incumbent in the general election. Fewer than 5% of the women who challenged incumbents for House seats in 1992 were victorious, despite the general momentum in favor of women during that year. On the state level, the pattern was not very different: 55% of women won when running for open seats, but only 12.6% succeeded in ousting incumbents.[33]

As discussed in Chapter 2, another factor that may complicate the situation for a woman is that family responsibilities often limit her window of personal opportunity. She may find herself well positioned politically to run for an open seat but be personally constrained, perhaps by young children, from taking the plunge.

In some parts of the country, voters have begun warming to the idea that more turnover is healthy for our political institutions: as of February 1996, 21 states had passed ballot initiatives limiting the terms of their state and/or federal lawmakers. However, the long-term success of the term limitation movement is by no means assured. Ballot initiatives have been rejected in Washington, Utah, Mississippi, Montana, North Dakota, Oregon, and Wyoming. In California, there is an aggressive legal challenge to Proposition 140, one of the nation's earliest and most stringent term limit measures.

More to the point, term limits are not generally understood— and have almost never been pursued—as a route toward gender parity. While organizations like the League of Women Voters and the American Association of University Women strongly advocate for women's public policy concerns, they have not been in the forefront of the term limits movement. On the contrary, the opposite is true: the League of Women Voters has actively supported various court cases aimed at blocking or overturning term limits.

In her provocative book *The Deep Divide: Why American Women Resist Equality,* Sherrye Henry makes the case not only for term limits but also for voter registration as a gender-equity issue. "Only 55% of the voting-age population cast ballots in 1992," she points out. "Because women vote in greater proportions than men, any registration drive, or any means of making the act of voting easier, is likely to benefit female candidates."[34]

Not only do women go to the polls in greater proportions than men—a pattern consistent in every national election since 1986—but they also register to vote in larger absolute numbers. For at least a decade, U. S. Census Bureau data has revealed a "registration gap." It is especially interesting to note that women voters outnumbered men by over 12% in 1994—an election dubbed by the media, because of its swing toward conservative Republicans, as the "Year of the Angry White Male."

The registration advantage is no secret to many women's groups. During 1996, a coalition of 110 organizations sponsored "Women's Vote '96," a nonpartisan grassroots campaign to ensure that female voters flexed their muscles at the ballot box. The success of this effort—women were largely credited with tipping the election

Table 4.1. A 10-Year "Voter Registration Gap"
(in millions)

	Female Registered Voters	*Male Registered Voters*
1994	62.7	55.3
1992	67.3	59.3
1990	60.2	53.0
1988	63.4	55.1
1986	59.5	52.2
1984	62.1	54.0

Source: Center for the American Woman and Politics, Eagleton Institute of Politics, Rutgers University.

to Bill Clinton over Bob Dole—enhances the likelihood that it will be repeated and institutionalized.

But structural changes hardly matter without large numbers of women to take advantage of them. Reflecting on the question of why there still seem so few female candidates, Mayor Susan Bass Levin offered, "Well, it's a hard life." I heard this phrase repeated so often it sounded like a mantra—or an oblique way of capturing many things that these women couldn't, or wouldn't, say. What remains unclear is whether political life is, on balance, harder for women than for men.

Regardless, some of the hardships are surely distinctive in nature, degree, or duration. Whether the rewards outweigh these difficulties is a judgment that must be made by female politicians individually—but hopefully with a sense of what it means for all of them collectively.

5
Beyond the Battlefield:
Challenging the Norms of Legislative Warfare

"I've got a woman's ability to stick to a job and get on with it when everyone else walks off and leaves it."
—Margaret Thatcher, former prime minister of England

"It is not that women are better than men...but I hope we all accepted long ago that we are different. The most sympathetic and sensitive of our men friends, no matter how hard they try, cannot hear with a woman's ear or process information through a woman's experience."
—Ann Richards, former governor of Texas

Barbara: "A Nice Do-Gooder Lady"

Her soft-spoken, unassuming style in private would probably come as a shock to the dozens of over-eager real estate developers she has faced down in public. As city council president in a large suburban municipality undergoing rapid expansion, Barbara has built a regional reputation for controlling growth with vision and firmness. But her firm hand can have a light touch; local newspapers also describe her as a careful and sympathetic listener who works hard at earning her constituents' trust. A well-known civic leader and president of the League of Women Voters, she had served on planning and zoning commissions but had no prior political experience when she decided to run.

"The local political establishment didn't know quite what to make of me," she recalls with a bemused shrug of the shoulders. "For one thing, I insisted on talking positively about the community rather than negatively about my opponent. And I refused to shoot from the hip; I still do. To me it's much more important to be thoroughly educated about an issue than to be able to reel off one-liners about it.

"I was so different from the typical politicians in town that they kept asking other people, 'Why is she running? What does she want?' They assumed that I needed a job, or that I just liked attention; it was inconceivable to them that a nice do-gooder lady like me would run for office just based on an interest in government."

While Barbara sailed easily to election, her plunge into the churning currents of daily political life gave her a shock. "Coming into this fresh from the League of Women Voters, I just wasn't prepared for the macho confrontational nature of it. My mode had always been consensus, cooperation, accommodation, harmonizing with other people to get things done. But the council meetings were like war games: the only way to score points was by torpedoing the opposition. It was my first encounter with a situation where people were actively encouraged to ridicule and undercut each other—they called it 'making a kill'—to get ahead."

Barbara adapted successfully, if not altogether comfortably. "There's a reason why politics is described as 'an arena'—it's because punching skills are valued more than people skills. By my second term, I had learned to thrust and parry with the best of them. But I still believe that I'm more effective at mobilizing and motivating people than at wrestling with them."

As evidence, Barbara recounts the biggest battle of her career, where she faced not a single developer but one of the largest and richest public utilities in the region. At issue was the utility's plan to construct a power plant near homes and schools in the heart of the city. To Barbara, this posed a significant public health threat, particularly to children.

The utility had vast financial resources and statewide political clout. Nevertheless, she first tried direct confrontation with its representatives. "When I demanded that they appear to justify the project at a public meeting, they showed up but simply stonewalled. Under the law, they were free to do just about anything they wanted, so I had very little leverage."

But Barbara had something else: strong ties to a large and vocal citizens' group. Led by public health advocates who were also mothers—and armed with evidence of a link between power plants and childhood leukemia—the group immediately agreed to help Barbara organize forums, rallies, and a massive grassroots effort. In a matter of weeks, she had mobilized thousands of people; the utility was engulfed in a tidal wave of community outrage.

At the time, Barbara was the most junior member of the city council. She notes that the more experienced officials took a detached approach. "They supported me on the issue—after it became obvious that the community was up in arms over it. But none of them ever developed the same fierce determination that I shared with the citizens' group."

Reflecting on that determination, Barbara acknowledges that there were many committed men as well as women involved during the course of the effort. "But I always thought it was interesting that the *leadership* was all female," she points out. "It's easy to glibly dismiss that, to say that women led this fight just because they had more time to attend meetings. But I'm convinced that it's also because issues of children's health resonate much more powerfully with women. The members of the core group sacrificed their personal lives for months. They were absolutely unwavering in the face of the utility's legal threats and a lot of heavyhanded pressure. I can't say that about some of the councilmen."

Eventually, the utility withdrew all of its original plans—a victory more complete than Barbara had dared to hope for. She is fully aware of the magnitude of this accomplishment. "During those times when I'm feeling low, and I start questioning whether I'm really cut out for politics, I remind myself that I'd probably be looking out my window at that power plant today if I hadn't been in office when it all happened. That's enough to keep me going!"

To what does she attribute her continued success in elective office? Barbara thoughtfully identifies three factors: "One, I try to out-argue my opponents rather than bludgeoning them. Two, I go out of my way to show people that I respect their opinions even when they're the opposite of mine. Three, I make a good-faith effort to bring people together, rather than driving them apart. Even though it's unconventional among politicians in this town, that approach has served me well; I've been reelected overwhelmingly three times."

However, Barbara suspects that being an unconventional politician is a double-edged sword. "The reality is, party leaders and many of the insiders who give money to candidates still look for a certain combativeness that goes beyond forcefulness or determination—it's more of an affinity for aggression itself."

During her years in office, she adds, "certainly I've seen some women in office who do have that characteristic, and I'm glad to see them move up. But we have a long way to go before any significant number of women like me can make it to the top of the ladder—with our people skills (and, yes, our femininity) intact."

Politics as Blood Sport

Geraldine Ferraro, former congresswoman and 1984 Democratic vice-presidential nominee, has observed that even in the crucible of political life, women continue to act less like their male counterparts and more like, well, women. "Instead of engaging in confrontation, women are more apt to negotiate," she recently wrote. "Instead of dealing in win-lose terms, women are more apt to see the gray area in between. Instead of thinking only of today, women are more apt to think in terms of the needs of generations to come."[1] When I asked them if they agreed with Ferraro, most of my interviewees nodded vigorously. Some, apparently wishing to steer clear of a stereotype, answered "no"—and then proceeded to describe themselves in words that almost precisely matched Ferraro's.

Maryland's Montgomery County Councilwoman Betty Ann Krahnke, for example, neither cultivates nor even acknowledges much of a "feminine" approach to politics. She is very much an individualist. (I met her the day after a major blizzard, when she had insisted on monitoring the county's snow-clearing operation—by riding a plow.) Nevertheless, she harbors not a doubt that a woman's life experience is a pivot for her policy viewpoints.

"Women take a longer view of most issues," she comments, in a tone she might use to say that the sky is blue. "We're dealing in our personal lives with both the younger generation and the older generation, so their needs are very immediate for us."

Many women believe this makes them more cautious than men. "We ask different kinds of questions, and often more of them. Women take the time to think about all the complex human dimensions of situations," mused Judy Knudson, former chair of the Board of Supervisors of James City County, Virginia. Observed New York

Assemblywoman Susan John simply, "Motherhood just seems to make women more risk-averse."

Knudson and others shared the uncomfortable feeling that their numerous questions might make them "look stupid" or engender resentment among colleagues for delaying the decision-making process. But it was a risk they thought worth taking. Recounted another local official:

> We'd been in negotiations for months with a company that wanted to build a waste-processing facility less than a mile away from the nearest homes. I kept asking about the potential air-quality risks to that population. The other councilmembers just thought I was being a pest—until the evidence came out about emissions from those plants carrying poisons like lead and dioxin. All of a sudden, they began referring to my concerns as "prudent" instead of "obstructionist."

Political confrontations, particularly in public view, can be unpleasant for anyone. However, many women suspect that politics is a blood sport because men like it that way. "We had a recent public meeting where the guys went at each other all night," reported Mayor Mickii Carter of Johnson City, Tennessee. "By the end, I was frazzled and exhausted. But as they were leaving, one of them turned to me with a big smile and said, 'That's the most fun I've had in ages!' I was startled—not because I can't be just as confrontational as this fellow when it's necessary, but because I don't enjoy it and I never look for a fight."

Middletown, New Jersey is a large and diverse suburban town of 70,000, known for its tough politics and contentious citizens' groups. Nonetheless, former mayor and three-term councilwoman Rosemarie Peters concludes that she is politically popular in part because of her low-key, nonthreatening mien—not in spite of it.

"I think voters appreciate when you're natural and sincere in your approach. That works to my advantage," says Peters. "And besides, I couldn't be like the guys even if I wanted to. Almost all of the men I've served with have been heavily involved in sports since their childhoods. Maybe that's why they seem to enjoy going out into the arena, playing hard, hitting hard—and then going out for a drink with a guy they just punched in the nose."

She laughs at the sobriquet "Steel Magnolia," but Georgia State Representative Kathy Ashe sometimes applies it to herself. A successful three-term veteran of numerous legislative battles, Ashe nonetheless expresses distaste for the "attack mode" she observes among most of her male colleagues: "I don't believe that someone always has to lose in order for anyone to win in the legislative process. The traditional destroy-the-enemy approach: that's not government, it's warfare."

Of course, belligerent behavior is not the sole province of men. Female politicians do plenty of sparring, with opponents of both sexes. But their stories call to mind an old adage: "Give a child a hammer, and everything needs pounding." To many women, bellicosity is the child's hammer of politics: the established male norm, but not always the most effective implement.

All of the women recalled situations where the only way to get results was to fight for them, aggressively and sometimes ruthlessly. No one approach, they agreed, was always best. But if women can learn the skills introduced to political life by men, shouldn't men be more open to those contributed by women?

Noted psychologist Sandra Lipsitz Bem argues that both genders can, and should, learn from each other to maximize human potential:

> An individual [can] be both masculine and feminine, both instrumental and expressive, both agentic and communal, depending upon the situational appropriateness of these various modalities; and...it is possible for an individual to blend these complementary modalities in a single act, being able, for example, to fire an employee if the circumstances warrant it, but to do so with sensitivity for the human emotion that such an act inevitably produces.[2]

Is there such a thing as androgynous behavior in office? One mayor offered an example. No man, she told me, could have been more hard-nosed in slashing public subsidies for her town's summer camp program, which was chronically over budget. She was denounced at public meetings, ridiculed in the newspapers, and even picketed at her home. But instead of counterattacking, she used a "motherly approach" to soothe worried citizens, vowing that no local child would go unsupervised. Over a 12-month period, she personally led a group of parents who solicited funds, equipment, and management advice from youth-oriented businesses. Reconstituted as a public-private enterprise, the camp became so successful that it is now cited as a model for others around the state.

On a loftier plane, observers of Secretary of State Madeline Albright (the first woman appointed to that post) have noted that she is often overtly feminine, even "flirtatious" on the job. At the same time, she can talk—and act—as tough as any other world leader. But Anita Perez Ferguson, president of the National Women's Political Caucus, points out that this combination of traits remains very rare on high levels and that it reflects Albright's personal sense of achievement, not an overall cultural change. Albright, born in Czechoslovakia, is "not eligible to be president of the United States, so she can relax and be who she is. There are very few other women in business or politics who have reached that point."[3]

Interactive Leaders

Research on women in management suggests that female leadership styles are often interactive and nonauthoritarian, unlike the command-and-control approach historically favored by men. In the traditional model, command-and-control leaders issue orders to subordinates, who are expected to comply or face punishment. Power derives from position rather than persuasion. Decision-making is rigidly hierarchical, and authority is rarely shared. Neither is the credit for success, which nearly always redounds to the greater glory of whomever resides at the top.

Perhaps because managerial women have so infrequently been at the top, they have shown a willingness to experiment with more participative styles, usually built around cooperation and consensus among workers at different levels. Based on her groundbreaking study of 456 female executives, management scholar Judy B. Rosener coined the term "interactive leadership" in 1990 to describe successful women who "encourage participation, share power and information, enhance other people's self-worth, and get others excited about their work."[4]

Rosener acknowledges that there are women who succeed by adhering to the traditional corporate model and some men who choose to lead in participative ways. But it is hard to argue with her observation that women's life experiences seem to prepare them particularly well for interactive leadership: "The fact that most women have lacked formal authority over others and control over resources means that by default they have had to find other ways to accomplish their work. As it turns out, the behaviors that were natural and/or socially acceptable for them have been highly successful in at least some managerial settings."[5]

Rosener's work has not gone unchallenged. Some scholars suggest that leadership differences are more a matter of personality than gender. Also, not all of the behaviors associated with women in the workplace are positive or constructive ones: in her book *When Women Work Together,* author Carolyn Duff argues that women show greater tendencies toward jealousy, gossip, and back-biting.[6]

Still, more recent and exhaustive studies have supported Rosener's conclusions. One of these was a 1996 report with a question as its title: "Gender Differences at Work: Are Men and Women Really That Different?" Researchers Janet Irwin and Michael Parrault analyzed more than 900 executives on 31 behavioral measures—and then answered, resoundingly, "yes." Like Rosener, they found many of the differences to be advantageous to women in decision-making environments.[7]

Academic debate notwithstanding, Rosener's basic premise—that female leaders have an affinity for cooperation and consensus-building—has gained wide currency. So wide, in fact, that virtually all of my interviewees had heard of it in some fashion. More importantly, almost all agreed with it. Perhaps this was why some of them seemed a bit sheepish when they talked about themselves in similar terms. Did they think I'd be disappointed to find conventional behavior among pathbreaking women like themselves?

On the contrary, their stories suggest that interactive leadership remains far from conventional in politics, despite its common appellation as "the art of compromise." Apparently, not all politicians share the same definition of compromise. In Rosemarie Peters' words, "Compromise doesn't mean that you badger me into accepting that I'm wrong and you're right." Indiana State Representative Vaneta Becker used much the same language: "Compromise is supposed to be give and take—not my going along with whatever you want just because you're from a more powerful district."

In fact, genuinely cooperative efforts among politicians were cited as jewel-like bits of experience—valuable, memorable, and rare. When I asked women to describe incidents of teamwork (beyond party-line voting) or resource-sharing, for instance, many of them initially drew a blank. One responded bitterly, "Resource-sharing? Sure. I was told that if I didn't share my financial resources with a particular candidate, the party leadership would support someone against me in a primary next year."

Women's caucuses were an exception. Legislators who work regularly with these bodies, like Georgia's Kathy Ashe, are convinced that they succeed precisely, and solely, because of a strong cooperative spirit. Ashe acknowledges important partisan and ideological divisions among caucus participants: "But those differences are checked at the door of the Women's Caucus, where everyone understands that our whole purpose is to identify common turf. Unfortunately, that approach seems to break down in other spheres of the legislative process. I really believe that women in government work better across party lines, racial lines, and other dividers."

Ashe adds that as a leader of Georgia's Women's Caucus, she is sometimes teased by the men about why she doesn't demand a caucus for them, too. "The truth is, I think the men would be better off if they did work together on our model. But I don't believe they know how—or have any interest in learning."

Both Republican and Democratic women in Congress perceive similar distinctions. Says North Carolina Republican Sue Myrick: "Women tend to always try to find a solution. We aren't as confrontational as men. We team build. It gives us a definite advantage. We come into situations with a more relaxed, open attitude."[8] From across the aisle, Missouri Democrat Karen McCarthy agrees: "We're more inclusive. We tend to bring people into the scheme in the effort to create unity....Our egos are less domineering than men's."[9]

Council President Jo Ann Boscia of Lakewood, Ohio sees the matter of leadership style in broader terms. "In my experience, women and men use very different problem-solving frameworks. Many men come to the table with a traditional corporate mentality: their paradigm is 'business as usual.' Women are paradigm-shifters. We're good at managing change, and we're used to it. After all, between raising our kids and negotiating with our spouses, we get a lot of practice!"

"A Social Worker with a Little Power"

Does it matter who sites the traffic lights?

Talk to any local official about the relevance of gender to their jobs and they are likely to begin with a similar rhetorical question. It is hard to dispute that the process of delivering basic public services is gender-neutral; indeed, garbage trucks and parking meters are many people's only concrete representation of government.

But at any level, government must ultimately take on a human face—the face encountered by citizens when they seek to question or change how it operates. Here, according to many of the women I interviewed, is where gender often matters. They believe that they are accessible to their constituents above and beyond the call of duty, and this is a key point of pride.

The matter of accessibility intrigued me. I had already heard much about the pressure of public officeholding, most of it obviously generated by the needs and demands of individual constituents. And yet, while constituent service was emotionally draining as well as disproportionately time-consuming, almost every officeholder stressed the importance of maintaining an open door—and a sympathetic ear. As they shared stories of troubleshooting, helping, comforting, and above all listening, I understood that these tasks were a major source of professional satisfaction. Women go out of their way to be accessible not because of some mysterious feminine impulse but because citizens respond so favorably to it, and because they believe they do it well. A businessperson (or a political strategist, for that matter) might say they've found a market niche.

Positive feedback about attributes like listening skills spurs them on to still greater efforts. Rosemarie Peters of Middletown, New Jersey beamed with pride as she recounted the praise in a recent constituent letter: "The woman had attended one of our meetings, and she wrote, 'Just watching you on the dais, I could see that you really listened and you cared.' To me, that was the greatest tribute. It affirmed my whole philosophy about politics, which is that people vote for you because they sense that you're genuinely interested in helping them." To Indiana Representative Vaneta Becker, even the job of a state legislator boils down to listening and helping, one constituent at a time: "I see myself as a social worker with a little power," she said. "Cutting red tape, solving personal problems, getting answers for people—that's what makes government relevant to their lives."

When it comes to accessibility, it's hard to imagine outdoing Anita Hummer, mayor pro tem of Elizabeth City, North Carolina. During her first year in office, she felt intimidated about speaking up in council meetings: "I felt that you need a big voice and a big personality to be heard, and I have neither. So I spent that whole year listening....I listened to all kinds of people, who called me from all over town." She learned so much about community needs from these callers and was so emboldened by their feedback that she decided to start a call-in radio show, "Talk Back with Anita Hummer." Elizabeth City residents could now choose to share their concerns privately with Hummer or on the airwaves where they might also connect with other citizens.

Accessibility means formal workday policies like open office hours and regular visits to neighborhood centers. Often it encompasses informal commitments, too, such as taking constituent phone calls late into the night—seven nights a week—and even responding to the needs of people who vote in other districts. The pride women politicians take in such efforts is sometimes tinged with a bit of resentment. Understandably, a hardworking legislator like Virginia's Delegate Shirley Cooper is both flattered and wearied when another lawmaker's constituent calls her at 7 o'clock on Saturday morning because he's heard that she's unusually responsive: "I also know it's because he wouldn't dare get his own representative out of bed," she remarks ruefully. Another perspective: in Jackson, Mississippi, Councilwoman Marcia Weaver decided to run (unsuccessfully) for the state legislature out of sheer frustration "that my representative wouldn't return my phone calls!"

The need for "open government," where officials are accessible and decision-making is observable, preoccupies so many women that it is as if they perceive a conspiracy to keep the doors of government closed. In fact, modern procedural requirements make such a conspiracy implausible: secrecy is hard to maintain in the face of public bidding, budgetary disclosure, and so-called "sunshine laws" (which require elected officials to deliberate in public sessions).

But old suspicions die hard. Listening to the stories of women politicians, I could well understand why. Many had not been originally recruited, or even supported, by the traditional political establishments in their communities. Because it was so tough for them to break in, they recognize the importance (and certainly the public appeal) of easing access for others.

This was certainly the case for Mayor Mickii Carter of Johnson City, Tennessee. She was unable to recount the events that swept her into the political arena without revealing some of the old anger and bitterness:

> I first got involved with city affairs when I formed a group called Citizens for Responsible Government. We wanted to stop the city commission from siting a garbage dump 600 feet from a housing complex. Well, I attended public session after public session, but the commission members ignored me, humiliated me, and refused to let me speak. It took 200 members of my group, who came to City Hall and practically shut down their meeting, for them to grant me a few minutes at the microphone. When I ran for office, I vowed that if I did nothing else, I'd make sure that no citizen would ever have to go through that again.

The women politicians also act on a strong sense of what the public expect of them. Sometimes this is intuitive—"I just know that's what people elected me for"—but it can also be a calculated political appraisal. "I was the first official to call for public hearings at senior citizen centers all over the city," recalled a mayor. "I felt it was the right thing to do—but I also knew it would send my name recognition through the roof." Whether or not the emphasis on accessibility has anything to do with gender, these women believe it has everything to do with their success at the ballot box.

"Not on a Pedestal"

Accessibility was frequently mentioned together with approachability, but the two qualities are not the same. Officeholders can make themselves accessible simply by opening a door, but not all constituents will feel comfortable enough to venture through it. Some women consciously strive to augment that comfort level, especially among the very young and the very old in their communities. Others believe that it is automatically enhanced by their gender. "I've often thought that being a woman is a great advantage in that way," reflects Rosemarie Peters. "Both women and men naturally gravitate to women when they want to talk about things that have emotional resonance for them."

Part of being approachable, said several officeholders, is being seen "not on a pedestal" but as an ordinary person with the same responsibilities and frustrations as everyone else. Mayor Susan Bass Levin of Cherry Hill, New Jersey commented that residents can hardly feel intimidated when they encounter her as "just another mom in the supermarket checkout line." Says Delaware State Senator Patricia Blevins, "People feel I'm more approachable than other legislators because where they usually see me is at PTA meetings, not at the statehouse."

In the course of my research, I interviewed women in offices, conference rooms, restaurants, hotels, and occasionally in their homes. The settings were sometimes excessively formal or uncomfortable, and circumstances could be awkward—as when I arrived early for a home interview and embarrassed a sleepy mayor in her bathrobe. But no matter where we were, or what time of day or night, all of the officeholders went to great lengths to put me at ease. They proffered food and drink, showed interest in my work, and exhorted me to "make yourself at home." Even those with the loftiest titles insisted that I address them by their first names.

At first I attributed these behaviors simply to courtesy shown a stranger who has come a long way. But then I watched how they treated other visitors: over and over, I saw people with and without appointments—and with and without power—welcomed like old friends. If indeed these women are more approachable than male colleagues, it isn't an accident but by design. They cultivate approachability as deliberately as any other political skill.

But it has its price. Women sometimes complained that male politicians get more respect, from the media as well as from the electorate, because they maintain an aura of importance and authority. "When you're always behind a big desk, nobody can see that you sit on your backside just like they do," was the earthy comment of a southern lawmaker. "I think that ordinary folks are in awe of a lot of the men in our legislature. People don't feel the same way about us women. I think that's healthy—except when it means they don't take us as seriously."

Indiana State Representative Mary Kay Budak described this scenario:

> Often I'm invited to attend town meetings together with the other representative and the state senator who serve my district. A reporter or a citizen will ask some question about a legislative issue and say, "Senator, how do you feel about that?" Then they'll ask the other guy, "Representative So-and-So, what's your opinion?" Finally they'll turn to me and say, "Mary Kay?" I go home and wonder why I don't get the same respect they do.

On balance, however, there is a consensus that women politicians make a difference by helping ordinary citizens feel that their opinions count. This consensus is buttressed by a national survey of male and female legislators conducted by the Center for the American Woman and Politics at Rutgers University: majorities of both women and men agreed that the increased presence of women has helped broaden citizen access to government, particularly among economically disadvantaged groups.[10] To Richmond, Virginia Councilwoman Viola Baskerville, this is so important that her staff is trained to use every constituent phone call as an opportunity for what she calls "citizen empowerment." Anyone who queries Baskerville's office receives both an answer to their question and a succinct but thorough recitation of how Richmond's city government works.

Interspersed with frequent—and perfectly logical—assertions that delivering basic public services is a gender-neutral job, I heard many indignant stories of women's concerns neglected or mishandled until a female official stepped in. Issues such as child welfare and domestic violence, I found, evoked strong emotion and a sense of special responsibility and competence even among those officials who insisted, "I don't want to be thought of as a woman—just as someone who's good at this job."

Mayor Joyce Savocchio of Erie, Pennsylvania fell into this category. For 15 years in office, she told me, she had made it a point never to draw attention to her gender. And yet, when her city was cited in 1992 for having the state's highest number of children living in poverty, she believes that being female gave her the extra credibility edge she needed to lead a massive reform effort. Particularly when it came to enlisting the help of the business community, Savocchio recalled, "it was critical for them to understand that this issue of child welfare had now become top priority for the city. That just seemed more believable coming from a woman than a man."

"I'm not a feminist. I'm a humanist," Mayor Mickii Carter hastened to tell me at the start of her interview. But when I asked her if she could describe some improvement in her city that wouldn't have happened without her, she responded immediately:

> Sure, I was able to get a special appropriation of $40,000 a year to support domestic violence programs. We'd had a shelter for victims of abuse, but it was just a warehousing facility. The idea of expanding it, to offer rehabilitative services to these women, had been on the table for nine years, but no one had done anything about it. The only change in nine years was that I was now sitting at the mayor's desk—and that was the only change necessary to get it done.

Women were also extremely sensitive to any real or perceived evidence of sexism, even when it had not personally affected them. For example, the travails of First Lady Hillary Clinton were a sore point even with some Republicans, who believed that she is held to an unattainable standard as both a traditional helpmate and a female professional (just like them!). Likewise, women of both parties cringed when I reminded them of the so-called Nannygate scandal that brought down U. S. attorney general nominee Zoe Baird: a few admitted that their own babysitting arrangements might not stand up to similar scrutiny. Why, they wanted to know, had *fathers* never been held accountable for child care?

In Colorado Springs, Councilwoman Lisa Are became indignant when she learned that elected officials could not be reimbursed for child care expenses associated with their jobs. Until 1995, she explained, council members were unpaid; this meant that a parent with responsibility for a young child—usually a woman—could not serve unless she was financially able to absorb the cost of child care. While Are's child had outgrown the need for such care, she vowed to change the rule "because it clearly discriminated against mothers." And although she did not often work closely with the other three women on the council, all of them joined her in a successful effort to designate child care expenses as reimbursable during official meeting times.

Partners in Change

Women legislators are more likely than men to report that citizens are very helpful to them, according to the Center for the American Woman and Politics.[11] At other levels of government, too, female officials find many ways to utilize the time and talents of ordinary people. It is interesting to consider the dynamics of this process. Do citizens take the initiative more readily with women, or are the women reaching out to them with greater frequency?

The current seems to flow both ways. Those officeholders with deep roots in nonpartisan civic organizations—over half of them—often mentioned that community activists seemed to trust them more than other elected officials. As mentioned earlier, there was also a consensus that women in government are generally more approachable than men.

It was perhaps more remarkable that many of the women regarded ordinary citizens, more than their fellow politicians, as natural partners in working for change. In fact, there were numerous instances where female officials actively recruited nonpolitical individuals or organizations to help them influence their own colleagues. "Someone once said the world is run by those who show up," reflects Georgia Congresswoman Cynthia McKinney. "What I've learned in politics is that it's possible to build a coalition of people who don't hold sway in Washington or Wall Street, and work toward the common goals of civil rights, equality of opportunity, tolerance, economic fairness and putting people before profits."[12]

Enlisting the support of people outside of politics has been a highly successful strategy for Mayor Karen Anderson of Minnetonka, Minnesota. She used it, for example, to push an affordable housing issue that precipitated a jittery reaction from the city council. She didn't take the councilmembers on by herself. Instead, "I got religious leaders involved, from throughout the area," she explains with great satisfaction. "They immediately saw the social justice side of the issue, as I knew they would, and asked their parishioners to write lots of letters in favor of it. Their fast response headed off most of the opposition before it could really build up steam and provided the political cover that some of the councilmembers needed in order to do what was right."

As a city alderman in Springfield, Illinois, Gwenn Klingler was branded by the other aldermen as "out to lunch" when she proposed the issuance of beer keg permits to combat teenage drinking. In response, Klingler mobilized her allies to show their support: schools, churches, Mothers Against Drunk Driving, and other community organizations. Her proposal passed.

There were similar stories of women reaching out to advocacy groups, neighborhood associations, PTAs—and often simply to old nonpolitical friends. "I think there's an absence of paternalism," said one lawmaker, "an appreciation that politicians don't always know best. That's why so many of us value and work hard at our grassroots relationships." On a less lofty but perhaps more telling note, another added: "Alliances among politicians are rarely based on anything but opportunism. Alliances with 'real' people usually have a lot more depth than that."

"We Just Work Harder!"

It was not only such grand themes as leadership style or the nature of politics that got women talking about their distinctiveness in elective office. One of the most frequent and most spirited observations was, in fact, quite mundane.

"We just work harder!" is a comment I heard around the country and on every level of office. There is some objective data to verify this perception, too. Actual reports by male and female elected officials of how much time they spend on legislative work (and how much they emphasize constituents' problems) have, indeed, revealed an imbalance.[13] But the women who brought this up were not always patting themselves on the back. They also saw in it evidence of weaknesses: self-doubt, unrealistic expectations, burnout.

Virginia State Senator L. Louise Lucas even poked a bit of fun at herself for being over-conscientious:

> During my first year in the Senate, I felt I needed every possible minute to prepare for every meeting. I couldn't focus on anything else until I had practically memorized the agenda. Well, late one night I was in my car on the statehouse grounds and decided I still wasn't ready for the next morning's session. So I pulled out a flashlight. There I was, studying the agenda by flashlight in the parking lot in the middle of the night, when two other senators pulled over to see what the trouble

was. They were astonished to see me just sitting there, studying away. And when they started to laugh at me, I had to laugh, too. It was such a ridiculous scene. But I felt that I had to be twice as good as anyone else just to start out even, and I've never quite gotten over it. That seems like a "woman thing"—why are we so hard on ourselves?

It is not an idle question. Several women admitted that self-criticism and self-doubt, more than external political circumstances, were holding them back from seeking higher office. Others believe that they could have run much earlier in their lives, if not for a debilitating fear of failure: not failure to discharge the public's business, but failure to live up to the traditional macho image of a tough-talking, hard-charging, take-no-prisoners warrior-politician.

Too, unrealistic expectations can lead to exhaustion and burnout. "We run ourselves ragged because we feel responsible for everything, and we try to be on the job 24 hours a day," says Pennsylvania's Bucks County Commissioner Sandra Miller. There were also women whose political ambitions were being consumed by the very burning passions that fueled their launches into office. "I didn't get into this to end up pushing papers at city hall, but to accomplish some policy goals," said one of these women disgustedly. "I'll give it a try for one more term; but if I can't make any more headway, I intend to quit and continue my work in advocacy organizations instead." Colorado Springs Councilwoman Lisa Are reflected that her life in the political arena has made her more, not less, appreciative of what an ordinary citizen can accomplish outside of it. "As an elected official, you're pushed and pulled by all these competing interests. I do a radio program called 'Answering Life's Challenges,' which allows me to address topics that are really important to people, like alcoholism, aging, finding balance in your life,...and sometimes I think I accomplish as much through that program as I do on council."

Another nearly universal lament: "We're not good at tooting our own horns!" Women shook their heads over their own reluctance to "lunge for the credit," as one legislator put it. While humility may be a virtue, New York Assemblywoman Susan John explained how it can also be a drawback:

Women are much more about building consensus, and less interested in credit or titles or getting their egos taken care of. That's good when it helps achieve certain policy objectives, and certainly it sometimes does. But it can hurt in terms of political advancement. We're just not as concerned with pushing our way to center stage, and that can mean that we get overlooked in the lineup for nominations or support to run for higher office.

New Mexico legislator Mimi Stewart adds that women's willingness to take a back seat can keep them from legislative leadership, too. "The guys feel like they deserve committee chairmanships as soon as they set foot in the statehouse. We women are much slower to jump at those opportunities, willing to spend much more time working quietly in the background." Missouri State Representative Nancy Farmer observes much the same thing. However, she points out that the eight-year legislative term limits recently enacted in her state (and under consideration in others) may herald a change. "In general, we've not been driven by our egos to rush right into the competition for leadership; we've taken our time thinking about what we like and what we're good at. But the term limits will force a change in our approach. I think more women will decide early to pursue a leadership track—because they'll realize it's now or never."

On Illinois' Kane County Board, Penny Cameron got tired of hand-wringing about women's humility and decided to do something about it. Active in a group called Women in Management, which brings together female decision-makers from both business and government, she talks proudly of helping to establish the group's "Promote Yourself Jar." "The idea is to donate money for a young woman's scholarship every time a member has accomplished something significant and feels like bragging about it," Cameron explains. "It teaches us to think of self-promotion as a positive thing instead of as an embarrassment."

Women also felt strongly that a back seat is better than none. For example, in her quest to enact a certain land use proposal in Minnetonka, Minnesota, Mayor Karen Anderson purposely allowed her male colleagues to "get their initials on it"—even though this meant obscuring her own contributions. Only by giving them some of the credit, she believes, was she able to get their interest and solidify their support. "I just said, 'Fine, if that's what it takes to get this done, then I'll do it!' " She suspects, though, that "in the larger picture, that strategy probably works to our disadvantage. I don't see a lot of men giving *us* credit we haven't asked for!"

The Ultimate Goal: Balance

Above all, female officeholders seek balance: between their political and personal lives, between modes of behavior, among the vast array of public issues that affect them as women and as citizens. They compete in a world of militaristic norms established by generations of men, even as their constituents look to them for the qualities traditionally ascribed to women.

In no other role is a woman buffeted simultaneously, and in full public view, by such powerfully symbolic waves of tradition and of change. For an individual to stay afloat in the crosscurrent takes strength and luck. For women as a group to break free of it takes numbers.

This is not only because female officials are more likely to target women's concerns when they are more than a token minority, though that is very important. Political scientists have also found that when women serve in state legislatures with significant numbers of other women, they exert more influence over their male colleagues.[14] In the same vein, local officeholders talked of feeling less inhibited about raising such issues as child care when they were not the only mothers in the council room.

It is also because a woman alone, or nearly alone, can become a lightening rod for negative stereotypes that undermine her morale and effectiveness. Councilwoman Adele Smith of Ogden, Utah is one of those who finds herself in such a predicament:

> As the only woman, I have to be careful in council meetings; I can't say whatever I want or as much as I want, because people will call me "that troublemaker," "the bitch," or "the woman who talks too much." When I recently gave a one-and-a-half minute explanation to a developer about why I didn't support his project, he wrote a letter to the editor complaining about my "10-15 minute tirade." Everything I do

gets magnified in importance, because I'm the only woman doing it.

Cognizant of such problems, women's advocates in recent years have looked to the political parties to recruit, train, and encourage larger numbers of female candidates, especially at the start of the pipeline. The next chapter will explore how effectively the parties, and other groups, are doing so.

6
Crashing the Parties:
Of Business, Bosses, and Back Rooms

"Find your sisters and brothers....
They will support you when you are on your way."
—Peter Gabriel, "Shaking the Tree" (Geffen Records)

Laura: From Poster Girl to Pariah

After a decade as one of her community's most visible environmental activists, Laura was pleased and not really surprised when representatives of her political party recruited her to run for a seat on the county commission. "I was known throughout the area for my professional expertise, and I'd been in demand for years as a public speaker," she explains. "I'd had no political experience, but it seemed logical that the party leaders would want me because of those strengths."

At first, it certainly seemed so. Once she had agreed to run, the party's literature was rewritten to showcase her accomplishments; at a kick-off reception in her honor, she was lauded for bringing "a unique dimension" to the campaign. There was only one problem: "I guess I was more 'unique' than they bargained for," she recalls ruefully. "I was the first candidate in 10 years who had not come up through the ranks, and it showed."

Laura had always been proud of her eloquence and outspokenness. She felt confident that these attributes were appreciated by the public, and they had been roundly praised in the press. But within the party organization, she soon realized that the same qualities simply raised eyebrows—and hackles.

"From the start of the campaign, I was careful to discuss my ideas with the party chairman and the other candidates on our ticket before voicing them publicly. I was still under the impression that I'd been recruited at least partly because of my reputation as a speaker. But it soon became clear that the others just thought I was

111

hogging the spotlight. I overheard one of my running mates complaining that 'she'd be okay if she'd just learn to shut up.' "

Laura will never forget the first time she gave a speech to a gathering of major party contributors. "The room was filled with lawyers, political appointees, and businessmen who seek out government contracts—people who look to the party, in one way or another, for their livelihoods," she explained. "At first they seemed attentive. But as soon as I brought up all my new proposals for county legislation, I could see their eyes starting to glaze over. It got worse by the minute; people were shifting in their seats and looking at their watches. After about ten minutes, the party chairman interrupted me to make a joke about longwinded speakers. By that time I'd gotten the message, and I stopped—to everyone's all-too-obvious relief."

Laura still couldn't figure out exactly what was wrong, however, and the situation worsened. "Things got so bad that as soon as I'd stand up to speak, I could see people rolling their eyes," she remembers painfully. "Finally one of the precinct leaders took me aside and said, 'Laura, these people respect you. But all you keep talking about is how much you want to change things. Remember that most of them have been through a lot of campaigns, and they've heard a lot of promises. Whether you keep those promises or not isn't what really matters to them. They just want to be reassured that you'll return their phone calls—fast.'

"Well, the light finally went on. From that moment, all I talked about to party regulars were the traditions I wanted to carry on, never the changes I hoped to make. My new speeches were very short and barely recognizable to anyone who'd known me before. But they worked: suddenly I was the party's poster girl again instead of a pariah.

"For the benefit of others," offers Laura, "here's what I learned: the engine that drives political parties, at least financially, is the opportunity to do business. In my experience, a lot of influential people in the party want their candidates to win not because those candidates are brilliant or eloquent, but because it'll get them contacts in high places, government work, patronage appointments. There's nothing wrong with that, and it's not incompatible with ideology or community spirit. But it's a culture shock for someone new."

Laura concludes, "You know why party organizations are called 'machines'? Because they mold, shape, and sometimes crush the candidates who represent them."

Diane: Who's Running the Show?

Unlike Laura, Diane was a party stalwart who had stuffed envelopes, knocked on doors, and run fundraisers for many previous candidates. She believed strongly that party organizations are critical to build identity, create accountability, and reward loyalty. She was especially proud to be part of a sizable group of women who had worked their way up the party ladder to positions of influence.

In fact, Diane had been elected to serve as president of the party's Women's Club, a group that had moved beyond its traditional social functions to establish some clout in recent years. While the Women's Club president did not play a role in the actual selection of candidates, Diane was regularly included in campaign strategy sessions. She and other club leaders were called upon to help draft position papers and press releases on issues of particular concern.

So, when she decided to enter a contested primary for a state senate seat, Diane had every reason to count on the Women's Club as her power base. "For one thing, the club was the fastest growing segment of the party, largely because of all my membership recruitment," she explained. "For another, I'd always encouraged independent thinking among us, and particular attention to female candidates."

Diane discovered that her vision of an independent-thinking bloc of women was really a mirage.

"The problem was that although I'd been active for such a long time, the guy I was challenging had been a force in the party even longer," she admits. "A lot of people saw that he was out of step with the electorate, but they owed him favors. And he was a big financial contributor, too. I thought I'd built up enough 'sweat equity' to compete with him on that basis, but I was wrong.

"It didn't take long for me to find out that the party leaders wanted me to back down. They put the word out that if I really cared about the good of the party, I'd withdraw from the race.

"Well, a serious split developed among the rank and file. My opponent and I were lobbying anyone and everyone we could. I knew he was making inroads by emphasizing his support among the leadership." But Diane believed that the Women's Club was her ace in the hole; not only would the club's endorsement give her more legitimacy and a boost in morale, it would also bring her some of the most experienced campaign workers and committed volunteers in the party.

Finally came the day when the Women's Club convened to hear from both candidates. Diane was nervous but continued to feel confident even when she saw that the party leaders who opposed her had made a special point of attending the gathering. Not until later did she learn that they had also phoned almost every member of the audience to lobby against her the night before.

She knew the battle was lost as soon as she finished her speech. "They were afraid even to clap for me," she recalls with more sadness than anger. "As I left the podium, all I heard were women clearing their throats—the same women I had worked with and befriended and counted on for 10 years.

"I'll never know whether they truly believed that he was the better candidate, or whether they had simply been intimidated by all the pressure," Diane adds. "But either way, I got a very clear message about who still runs the show—and how few women, even in a strong party organization like mine, are willing to take, or demand, an independent role."

Ladders or Anchors?

Since at least the late 1970's, when female candidates began to emerge in more than token numbers, party loyalty and service have been viewed by political scientists as tickets to success for ambitious women. After all, women have hardly been strangers to party organizations; decades before they began stepping forward to run, they were omnipresent as campaign volunteers—making coffee, licking stamps, ringing doorbells, and performing all manner of menial but critical tasks. Through sheer hard work and persistence, some women were attaining leadership posts in both the Democratic and Republican parties long before much of the electorate was ready to accept them as candidates. In fact, a massive tracking study of 3000

California political activists from 1964 to 1986 found that in most years women were more likely to hold offices within the party structure than men.[1] There has never been a female chair of the Democratic National Committee, and a woman led the Republican National Committee only once, during the Watergate years (Mary L. Smith, R.N.C. chair 1974-1977). Nevertheless, as early as 1972 the national presidential nominating conventions of both parties featured sizable percentages of female delegates: 40% at the Democratic convention, 32% at the Republican convention.[2]

Ten years later, a leading political observer noted that women were in charge of most political and administrative functions behind the scenes at the Democratic National Committee. On the G.O.P. side, women comprised more than half of the party's top strategists.[3]

In 1994, soon-to-become House Speaker Newt Gingrich received much of the credit for the G.O.P.'s sweep of the House of Representatives. But responsibility for the nuts and bolts of the massive national operation was entrusted to six women staffers at the National Republican Congressional Committee. Led by Executive Director Maria Cino, described as "the antithesis of the men in suspenders who run this town," these savvy female operatives were put in charge of national advertising, political strategy, and a $4.5 million debt. "Placing so many young, little-known women in top posts didn't sit well with some party regulars," reported the *Wall Street Journal*. But when they succeeded in retiring the debt as well as masterminding a historic electoral turnaround, the skepticism turned to adulation in G.O.P. circles.[4]

Despite such gains, party leaders have repeatedly been accused by scholars of actively or covertly discouraging women from running for office—except in situations where no man will accept the party's nomination. "The failure of the parties to nominate women cannot be attributed to the lack of qualified women candidates," wrote political scientist Mary Lou Kendrigan in 1984. "If qualifications are measured in terms of age, occupation, education, training and interest, there are far more qualified women available than have been nominated. Discrimination appears the only factor that can explain the scarcity of women who are nominated by their political parties."[5] While more up-to-date research finds little evidence of such discrimination, parties are not yet off the hook. The lingering suspicion among academics is expressed in a 1995 college text, *Women, Politics and American Society,* which notes that "women are still disproportionately encouraged to run in unwinnable races or where the seat is a 'woman's seat,' that is, one previously held by a woman."[6]

The role of parties is also being scrutinized by women's advocates abroad. The Inter-Parliamentary Union, which represents 135 freely elected governments, reported in 1997 that while women are close to half of the global population, they hold fewer than 12% of all seats in the world's 179 parliaments. The increase in female representation since 1995? A dismal 0.4%. Why? The group's leaders pointed a finger at party organizations: "To get elected you have to become important in the party...and not enough women manage to do that," said Tunisian official Faiza Kifi. Added the author of the report, "Women must first achieve equitable power within political parties if they are to close the gap in parliament."[7]

So, troubling questions persist. Is there discrimination, or not? Do parties more often provide ladders to the top—or anchors to the bottom? Simple theories fade in the glare of complex, contradictory realities.

"None of the Old Boys Were Interested"

I heard only a few references to overt discrimination, and most of those were oblique. For example, Mayor Alice Schlenker of Lake Oswego, Oregon, though a past president of her Republican Women's Club, believes strongly that ambitious women are still marginalized in her party when it comes to nominations for state or federal office. Asked how, she replies only, "pure 1950's male politics."

Stories of women offered "sacrificial lamb" nominations or "women's seats" were more numerous—and more direct. I was especially struck by the matter-of-factness of women who spoke of such experiences, and it must have showed: one legislator tilted her head quizzically and exclaimed, "I can't believe you're surprised!"

But I was surprised, when I repeatedly heard the same observation, expressed in nearly the same words, from experienced officeholders like Gwenn Klingler. An attorney, former school board president, and the sole female alderman in Illinois' capital city, Klingler still was convinced that she won her party's support to run for the state legislature only "because none of the 'old boys' were interested." Klingler learned that the party could not find anyone willing to challenge the incumbent legislator in her district. When she stepped forward, "everyone said I was crazy, that he couldn't be beaten. But if they'd thought otherwise, I would never have gotten the party nod." The incumbent unexpectedly dropped out of the race, and Klingler won.

What about "women's seats"? "Those are the ones with less power, less importance as stepping stones to higher office," says Pennsylvania's Chester County Commissioner Karen Martynick. Of course, that is not always the case. In states with two-member legislative districts, one seat may be informally reserved for a woman if another woman has previously held it. However, there is a catch: as one would-be legislative candidate told me bitterly, "Once the 'woman's seat' is filled, no one would dream of putting a *second* female on the ticket."

Most of the time, I found that women had not been actively discouraged by their parties from running for office—but they'd not been encouraged either. This was true among officeholders in both parties. For example, Republican Kathy Ashe, who represents an affluent section of Atlanta in Georgia's statehouse, would seem to have little in common with Democrat Mimi Stewart, state delegate from a diverse district in Albuquerque, New Mexico. But the receptions they received from their respective party organizations when they decided to run are disturbingly similar.

Ashe decided to run in 1991, after years as a community activist and legislative aide. "The party was simply appalled," recalls the legislator, now in her third term. "They just saw me as one of those nice do-gooder types who wasn't a lawyer and didn't fit the mold." Stewart was not only an experienced lobbyist for the New Mexico Teachers' Federation but also a ward and precinct chair for the Democratic party. Nonetheless, she says emphatically, "The party never encouraged me, ever! When I announced my candidacy in 1992, people told me I was just getting myself into trouble....It certainly wasn't the 'Year of the Woman' in New Mexico!"

It is easier to understand party indifference, even hostility, to a candidate who has purposely maintained a distance from local political leaders before running for office. This was the case for numerous women who had won election to nonpartisan local bodies on the basis of broad civic involvement, not partisanship. What struck these women, however, was the absence of interest or outreach from their parties even *after* they became established local officials.

It is particularly mystifying to Councilwoman Adele Smith of Ogden, Utah, who was the lone Democrat as well as the only woman elected to Ogden's city council in 1991. More importantly, her current position makes Smith, as she puts it, "the highest ranking female Democratic elected official in the county." And yet her relationship with the local party organization is only marginally stronger than it was before she got involved in city politics. "I've found the leadership very insular," she observes regretfully. "There's no grooming process, and I don't see them looking for talent outside of their own ranks." Oregon Republican Ellie Dumdi, well into her third term on the Lane County Commission, is more blunt: "For 10 years, the Central Committee (of the local party organization) has simply ignored me."

But at least the party has never stood in her way. According to Mayor Karen Anderson of Minnetonka, Minnesota, who describes herself as "an active longtime Republican," party activists recruited and supported one of her opponents in her re-election race. Another mayor approached party officials during her third term to discuss her interest in moving up to the county commission: "I was greeted with deafening silence," she reports. "It was as though I were some unknown supplicant off the street."

Penny Cameron, now a six-term member of Illinois' Kane County Board, vividly recalls her first primary:

> I remember that it was a Monday when I filed the necessary papers to declare my candidacy, knowing that no one else had stated an interest in running. But sure enough, by Thursday—two days before the deadline—the "old boys" had gotten together and found someone to challenge me. They said that because it was a primary, party representatives couldn't distribute my literature. But I saw them distributing *his* literature, clandestinely of course!

It is impossible to untangle gender from a myriad of other factors that may have been at work in such cases. But it is equally hard not to take note of their frequency: close to half of the officeholders described strained or indifferent relationships with their local party organizations, if not outright hostility.

Still, women like Laura do benefit from active party recruitment. Why, then, her sense of alienation even among people who clearly wanted her to win? And what of Diane, who spent a decade building a voice for women in her party, only to find that no one would raise it in her behalf?

The Business of Politics

Various studies spanning the years between 1979 and 1994 have repeatedly found that within groups of party activists, men evidence much more interest than women in the opportunity to make business contacts through party activity.[8] Conversely, most of the evidence suggests that women are more deeply anchored in their loyalty to the party. For instance, in the 20-year tracking study of 3000 California activists mentioned earlier, women were consistently more likely than men to report that they "have never supported a candidate of the opposing party" and to describe themselves as "one of those people who can be counted on to work for the party and its campaigns year after year, regardless of candidates."[9] The experiences of my interviewees breathed life into this data. At the same time, they revealed how these traditional modes of behavior can be smothering to women politicians.

"Especially on the local level, politics and business have become interwoven to the point where they're inseparable," says New York Assemblywoman Susan John. "And men still dominate business, especially the kinds of businesses that depend on government contracts." John sees this as a reason why so many women officeholders still enter public life via nonpartisan community work rather than party activism—and she believes they may pay a price for it. "I think that women who get elected to the legislature without strong party backgrounds sometimes are taken less seriously than the men for that reason. Coming up through the party system is seen as almost the same as coming up through a business, and that engenders a certain amount of respect."

Others echoed John's view. "Financial investments in the party pay dividends, in the form of patronage and loyalty," said one mayor. "If you're a businessman, there's nothing mysterious about this. But if you're not, it takes time to figure out all the relationships, and you can easily fall behind the guys who are already included in them."

Observers of national politics would find nothing awry in this picture. "Money [for campaigns] is not coming from ordinary Americans," reports the Center for Responsive Politics, an independent group that studies federal election financing. "American elections are paid for overwhelmingly by economically interested industries and a small handful of individuals."[10] But women like Laura are sometimes caught by surprise at the number and extent of such connections between business and politics even at the local level. More importantly, they can find themselves disadvantaged because they are neither known nor trusted by insiders who are most intensely concerned with an electoral outcome—because their livelihoods depend on it.

But, I asked, what about the *women* in business who use party connections to generate work? Aren't they making the environment more comfortable for female politicians? In response, more than one woman shot me a look that said, "You must be joking." In the experience of most, there are simply too few of such businesswomen in local political circles to make a difference.

Objective measures in this area are hard to come by. While there exist professional and occupational organizations whose members benefit substantially from public business (such as the American Bar Association; the National Association of Insurance Brokers; groups representing the building trades, civil engineering, and so on), these organizations typically do not maintain, or will not release, records of how many actually receive such business—and what proportion of those are women.

However, there are a few proxy measures that are suggestive, if imperfect. A U.S. Census Bureau study of economic activity between 1988 and 1992 shows that women far outpaced men in their rate of new business start-ups. But as recently as 1994, women-owned enterprises still accounted for less than 3% of all federal procurement dollars.[11] In a random check of how women have fared in procurement in three major cities during 1996, I found the following percentages of city contracts going to women-owned businesses: 4.5% in Philadelphia, 7% in Los Angeles, and 5-6% in Indianapolis.

My interviewees neither knew nor especially cared about such statistics. They had learned not to expect many women at the table when the menu of public business opportunities is served up. For instance, Commissioner Karen Miller of Boone County, Missouri observed matter-of-factly that three-quarters of her campaign contributors are real estate developers and building contractors but that there are virtually no women among that group. Miller's experience is striking because Boone County has enough female contractors to support their own professional association—but its members are invisible in local politics. "It's a catch-22," sighed one legislator. "You don't appreciate these things until you're an insider, but it's terribly hard to get on the inside unless you already understand them."

Sometimes it's not for lack of trying that party organizations put forth few viable female candidates: even active outreach efforts may turn up no recruits. Delaware State Senator Patricia Blevins has seen this firsthand. While she herself received no party encouragement to run for the legislature in 1990, she tries hard to encourage other women. Blevins is heartened by the recent blossoming of a Delaware Women's Democratic Club, but she admits that it has yet to produce a crop of new candidates. "A lot of women still find the whole idea very intimidating," she tells me with a discouraged shrug. "They think it's a lot more difficult than it is."

Or perhaps they see precisely how difficult it is. Absent a burning issue, a desire for self-aggrandizement, or the lure of business opportunities, some women apparently conclude that running to advance the party's collective interests just isn't worth the effort.

Women's Solidarity vs. Party Unity

Among women who are already party activists, one would expect a special bond, woven of shared ideological principles and reinforced by the broader cultural and political experience of womanhood. Indeed, such a bond often seems to exist. Illinois' Kane County Board member Penny Cameron, for example, relates that whenever a woman leaves an office in the local Republican party, she and other women take it upon themselves to identify an appropriate female replacement, "and we get together to insist on that appointment." According to Karen Miller, Boone County's Democratic female clerk is known throughout Missouri for her aggressiveness in promoting voter registration and political activism among women.

But the bond may fray just when a woman is counting on it most. The greatest strength of female activists—their unwavering party loyalty—can prove the Achilles' heel for a woman candidate who (in a primary or other interorganizational contest) opposes the choice of her party leadership. Her decision to challenge that choice may well be based on her perceived strength among women. But, as pointed out by committeewoman Rosemarie Peters of Middletown, New Jersey, a state with strong party organizations and notably low numbers of women in powerful offices, "The way to succeed in party organizations is by *not* being a rebel." To one would-be congressional candidate, this boils down to a simple trade-off: "When it comes down to women's solidarity versus party unity, the party wins every time."

It is a measure of how far political women have come that some, like New Jersey Governor Christine Whitman, are now the top—or only—choice of key party leaders in their states to run for the highest offices in the land. Others, like Congresswoman Sue Kelly and U. S. Senator Patty Murray, have successfully defied the powers-that-be, winning primary and even general elections without their wholehearted support. But these shining achievements are somewhat tarnished if party women are choosing to play only a limited role in them. Said one New Jersey officeholder who considers herself a staunch feminist as well as a great admirer of Governor Whitman: "It's absolutely fabulous that Christie won. And it's absolutely deplorable that she won in spite of, not because of, the degree of unity among women in the Republican party."

At least there seems to be more solidarity among women when it comes to supporting each other for less competitive offices. Commissioner Sandra Miller of Bucks County, Pennsylvania, for example, is convinced that she would never have been nominated by her party without the efforts of some hardworking women:

> When a spot on the county commission unexpectedly opened up due to a resignation, the party power brokers just couldn't agree on who to pick as a replacement. In fact, they were encouraging everyone and his brother to put themselves forward. When the executive board met, they selected three names—and even though I was well known in the party and definitely interested, mine wasn't one of them. But I had one other opportunity: the county committee, which includes all official party representatives from every election district, was also empowered to make an endorsement. I decided to go that route.

> I was part of a group of women who were the hardest workers in the party, although none of us qualified as power brokers because we couldn't bring in big donations. We all sat down together and laid out a strategy for working the county committee. Basically, every woman took responsibility for a certain number ofcmembers, whom she called and lobbied on my behalf. It was a huge project, but we were determined to do it because it was my only chance. When we succeeded, the guys couldn't figure out how in the world we had pulled it off!

However, for every Sandra Miller I always found a Martha Wong. While the experience of this Houston, Texas councilwoman with Republican women's groups was generally positive, she also had this to say: "I found out that these groups encourage women to work in campaigns, but not necessarily to run for office. It's encouragement of women to take more helping positions, not more public leadership positions."

Since local party leaders are so often described as playing a pivotal role in candidate screening and selection, I found myself wondering how many of such leaders are women. Granted, female leaders do not necessarily favor female candidates. However, their presence may serve as a barometer of cultural change within local party organizations. This has been true on the national level, where women in both parties have influenced the norms of behavior as well as the substance of discussion at recent presidential nominating conventions. For example, to many television viewers the most memorable image of the 1996 Republican convention was that of Maine Senator Olympia Snowe, working the airwaves in a lonely quest to change her party's position on reproductive choice.

In the 1980's, the role of national, state, and local parties in candidate recruitment and financing became more aggressive and central than ever before. At the same time, tightened state election regulations had the effect of channeling even more activity through the parties. These trends prompted one observer to comment that "the party game is now the only game in town."[12] If this is so, women have an interest in holding a proportionate share of the cards—whether or not they bet those cards on other women.

Local party structures differ, and titular leaders may have widely divergent levels of power and influence. That said, it seems reasonable to look at local leadership by women across states as an indicator of general trends. To do this, I selected 14 states at random and requested lists of county chairpersons from both the Democratic and Republican parties. The chart below summarizes my findings.

In five of these states, three out of four local party leaders (both Democrat and Republican) are still men. In over half, women are fewer than one out of three. Undeniably, women in party organizations have come a long way; after all, these numbers compare favorably with such measures as women's presence in state legislatures (21%). But they still reflect inequality—especially considering that women have been in the party pipelines for much longer than they have been running for office.

These findings elicited some telling reactions among the women I interviewed. For one thing, not one of them was surprised. Mayor Susan Bass Levin of Cherry Hill, New Jersey, whose state had the lowest percentages of female county chairs in both parties, pointed out that despite a tradition of having both a male and a female

Table 6.1. Women as Local Party Chairs
(% by State)

	Democratic	*Republican*
California	27	16
Colorado	35	25
Connecticut	22	20
Florida	32	26
Georgia	24	20
Illinois	15	12
Massachusetts	32	20
Michigan	40	30
Nevada	26	11
New Jersey	5	0
Ohio	17	16
Oregon	40	28
Pennsylvania	29	27
Texas	29	33

Note: In Massachusetts and Connecticut, local parties are organized primarily on a municipal level. All other state percentages apply to county party units.

leader in each county, "In my experience, it's almost always the man who's chair and the woman who's vice-chair, and their roles are different. The man is the front person, interacting with elected officials and community leaders and putting deals together. The woman does the administrative work, which is also very important but it's done in the background." I asked Levin if she thought it would make a difference for female candidates if there were more female party chairs. "It certainly couldn't hurt!" she laughed—and then added more soberly, "For the most part, candidates are hand-picked by either county chairmen or entrenched incumbents. Naturally, they're most often picking people they know and feel comfortable with—who are usually men like them."

Levin also described situations where women were considered for nominations but rejected because they lacked a base and fundraising experience: "But the guys who were picked didn't have a base or fundraising experience either." Assuring me that many of her own key party boosters are men, Levin spoke without rancor, and her expressive shrug suggested that women might as well make peace with the inevitable.

In Sandra Miller's opinion, "Women seem less attracted than men by the power of being party leader. Also, being the chair can cost money. You have to drive around a lot, take people out for meals or drinks, sometimes contribute to the cost of a headquarters. Where I've seen women as county chairs is in small counties where the local organization isn't very active."

Whatever the reason, at least one study supports Miller's contention that party leadership is less appealing to women than to men. Among 265 female and male party activists in Georgia, over half the women were "definitely not interested" in holding party office, compared to only 27% of the men.[13]

Miller's Republican counterpart in a neighboring Pennsylvania county is Karen Martynick, who observed that there had been only one female chair anywhere in the southeastern part of the state. "That area is our traditional power base—and she wasn't even invited to meetings of the other southeastern chairmen. I don't know why, but you can draw your own conclusions."

Martha Wong's story of running for tax assessor in Houston exposes the tip of another iceberg. Even when party leaders are supportive, they may lack control over other key individuals who are not. These informal opinion leaders or power brokers may exert enormous influence from within the proverbial—but very real—"back room."

"The woman who is local Republican county chair is the one who got me into politics," says Wong. But this chairwoman could not stop an onslaught against Wong by another powerful Republican who functions outside Houston's official party structure. "He is an extremely conservative individual, who picks his own slate and then organizes phone banks and mailings to support it. Even though I'd won 45% of the vote in a primary with six candidates, he refused to endorse me and I lost in the runoff—along with every other woman who ran in that election."

It is in part a measure of these problems that so many women are banding together in new party affiliates with the sole purpose of boosting female candidates. For example, Mayor Levin helped to start an organization of Democratic women in New Jersey called PAM's List (Power and Money). Building on the success of the oldest and best-known partisan women's fundraising network, EMILY's List (Early Money Is Like Yeast), PAM's List not only raises money for female legislative candidates but also creates "a place where Democratic women can meet and talk and encourage each other to run." G.O.P. women in New Jersey can come together, too, under the aegis of Republican Women of the 90's, or GROW (Greater Roles and Opportunities for Women), both inspired by the national G.O.P. organization WISH (Women in the Senate and House).

However, party-affiliated women's groups may operate within limits that are frustrating to some of their members. For instance, there may be a policy against supporting a woman in a primary fight—even when she is the only woman running. Instead, groups that maintain this policy (formally or informally) encourage female candidates to enter races without interparty contests; they also raise incremental funds for those women who survive the primary gauntlet without their help. These are important functions. But party primaries are still the starting gate for most prestigious, powerful offices, particularly when a seat is open (that is, without an incumbent to face in the general election). A disgruntled candidate who had withdrawn from a legislative primary—partly because no help was forthcoming from party-affiliated women's groups—put it this way: "The message is, we support women, but only when they're not running against men. Sure, it's a way of getting women to the table, but only for the leftovers."

Be that as it may, the proliferation of such party affiliates suggests that they are meeting a real need: by 1997, these groups had cropped up in at least eight states, sometimes in both parties. At the same time, women are also joining hands across parties to offer encouragement with fewer strings attached.

Mayor Mickii Carter of Johnson City, Tennessee is a founder of a new chapter of the bipartisan National Women's Political Caucus. A committed Republican, she nonetheless comments: "My feeling is that neither party is meeting the needs of women. That's why we're stepping outside of the party structures. It's the only way for us to focus on what we have in common as women. We can be such a tremendous force for change if we just stick together!"

Virginia State Senator L. Louise Lucas is an equally committed Democrat, but she takes time out of an impossibly busy schedule to serve on the board of Make Women Count. "It's the best thing that's ever happened to us," she says of the organization that recruits and trains female candidates, in both parties, for offices at all levels in her state.

These efforts may also be informal—even clandestine. A handful of free spirits told me that they had openly supported a woman of the opposite party in at least one election, but most of the time any such activity takes place behind the scenes. And usually it is local, involving a nonpartisan town council or county-level seat. But there were also small numbers of Democratic women in New Jersey who helped mobilize others to vote for Republican Governor Christine Whitman, just as some California Republicans worked hard for the election of California Senator Dianne Feinstein.

Still, the majority of women politicians are less comfortable crossing party lines than reaching out to other women in nonpartisan advocacy, educational, or social organizations. They have had considerable success and a few notable disappointments.

"A Man without a Country"

Women have often lacked the occupational experiences and networks that prepare individuals to run for public office. The unique role of nonpartisan women's groups like the League of Women Voters, the American Association of University Women, Business and Professional Women, and many others has been to help them bridge this gap. By encouraging personal activism and developing leadership skills, such groups have kindled and nurtured political ambition in many women who might otherwise have suppressed it. As early as 1983, a nationwide study of women in state legislatures found that fully half of them were members of the League of Women Voters.[14] Three-quarters of all female legislators have been found to belong to one or more national women's groups.[15] Across all levels of office, larger proportions of women than men have credited a non-party-affiliated organization, usually a women's group, with helping convince them to run.[16]

In keeping with these findings, almost all of my interviewees had at some time been very active with women's advocacy groups or with an occupation-related women's association (often with many at once). Several commented that they had been "hopelessly" intimidated by politicians and afraid of public speaking prior to their experiences in these groups. A number of women who are now serving third and fourth terms in office told me that despite the large numbers of partisan supporters they have cultivated over the years, their innermost circle of advisors and confidantes is still made up of old friends from the League of Women Voters. But political women sometimes expect more of these organizations than their members are willing (or able) to give.

One problem is inherent in the very nature of nonpartisan women's groups: most do not endorse candidates and cannot or will not act collectively to promote even a candidate from their own ranks. Of course, this does not preclude individual members from getting involved in political campaigns, and many do. But politicians like to think in terms of organized and visible blocs of support. Loose networks of friends from one or more organizations rarely inspire the same degree of confidence.

Still more frustrating to political women is what they see as a stubborn and naive refusal by some members of women's organizations to "get their hands dirty" with the nitty-gritty of political campaigns. "They think they can influence politics by staying above it," complained a former League of Women Voters president. A few women, who had tried unsuccessfully to recruit campaign volunteers from PTA's, garden clubs, church auxiliaries, and the like, hinted at a larger problem: "Most women have finally realized that they have a stake in public policy. But politics is still viewed as something nice girls don't do."

Indeed, with only a few exceptions (notably the National Organization for Women), even the most policy-oriented women's organizations have not worked very hard at getting their members to participate in political campaigns, for candidates of either gender, or to run themselves. Importantly, this may be different on a local chapter level. For example, Penny Cameron made certain during her term as a local president of the AAUW that any member's candidacy was announced at meetings and publicized in the chapter bulletin. When she ran for the Kane County Board, AAUW colleagues provided staunch and early support.

But national priorities are something else. Looking back over a year's worth of publications from the League of Women Voters, AAUW, and the Junior League, for example, I found a wealth of educational material about voting, citizen advocacy, and how government works. But there was relatively little discussion of how grassroots *political campaigns* work, and even less of a focused effort to develop women's candidacies. Fortunately, some changes are afoot: for example, the League of Women Voters announced at the end of 1996 that it would distribute a guide to running campaigns during 1997. The fall 1997 issue of *Outlook*, AAUW's national publication, included a feature entitled "Women in Power: The Lure of Elected Office."

Also, an argument can be made that the major nonpartisan women's groups ought not dilute their traditional focus on education, voluntarism, and other worthy, nonpolitical activities. But it is hard not to see a missed opportunity. Taken together, the League of Women Voters and the AAUW have close to a quarter-million members. If just one-tenth of 1% of these women had run for the U.S. House of Representatives in 1996, they would have more than doubled the number of female congressional candidates. How might such organizations do more to encourage and draw attention to member candidacies without crossing the line of nonpartisanship? One simple way would be to regularly include a list of such candidates in their national publications, indicating the offices they are seeking, their party affiliations, and their importance to the membership as a whole.

Commissioner Karen Martynick of Chester County, Pennsylvania raised another concern. "I was recently invited to a dinner following a golf outing for community leaders; there were 135 men and me," she related with some chagrin. "I knew a lot of them and I could certainly handle the situation. But what struck me is that all these men had spent a whole day together networking and bonding, making political contacts and pushing issues that are important to them. Women just don't do that kind of thing—at least not enough to catch up to guys who have been doing it for generations."

But it was Rosemarie Peters who most effectively captured the difficulty of reconciling a politician's perspective with the constraints and concerns of most women's nonpolitical world. She was only half-joking when she said, "Sometimes I feel like a man without a country."

7
No Cleavage During Speeches*: The Do's and Don'ts of Appearance, Behavior, and Political Etiquette

In Warwick, Rhode Island, recently, a cabdriver offered his opinions on GOP Representative Claudine Schneider's chance of unseating Democrat Claiborne Pell, a 30-year veteran of the Senate. He hasn't decided if he can support a woman. "Claudine's okay," he says. "But tell her to do something about that hair."
—News report, Business Week, October 1990

A former state Democratic Party chairman suggested to [Lynn] Yeakel, the Democratic Senate nominee in Pennsylvania, that her major qualification for office was her breasts.
—News report, Business Week, October 1992

When asked about the political intentions of Linda Smith, the Republican congresswoman from southwest Washington, Snyder [Democratic leader of the Washington Senate] undergoes a dramatic physical transformation. His voice grows deeper and stronger as he proclaims Smith "a self-promoting miserable bitch."
—News report, Seattle Post-Intelligencer, January 1996

Representative George Brown (D., California) chided his Republican opponent, Linda Wilde, for wanting to kill the Department of Education. "I imagine Linda, because she is a lady, is afraid of math," Mr. Brown said.
—"Thanks for the Memories," a collection of quips and quotes
Wall Street Journal, November 1996

---

*from the title of an article about campaign training for women, New York Times, August 1996.

131

> *New York City's elected Democratic officials and normally Democratic union leaders seem to be in a race to see who can put the most distance between themselves and [Manhattan Borough President] Ruth Messinger's campaign for mayor....Is the problem here sexism?* "I wouldn't say that on the record," said a woman who is both an elected official and a Messinger backer. "But off the record, of course it's sexism. Are you crazy? I've had people tell me they won't support her because she isn't attractive. They're going to vote for Rudy Giuliani because Ruth Messinger isn't good-looking enough for them."
>
> —"Editorial Notebook," *New York Times,* July 1997

Alison: It's All in the Eyes

As Alison remembers it, the incident couldn't have happened at a more difficult time. She had entered the home stretch of a tough and bitter re-election race. After months of fending off personal attacks and charges of financial impropriety by a female challenger, the tide finally seemed to have turned in her favor. But with only one week left before election day, she was under enormous pressure to use every minute effectively.

The day before her final debate, she was approached by a supporter who insisted on an immediate private meeting with her. "If he had not made it sound so terribly urgent," she relates, "I would never have agreed to meet with him at that point in the campaign. But he claimed that he had information I would need to perform at my best in the debate." So, Alison eked out a precious half hour from her schedule for the meeting, bringing along her campaign manager and issues director in anticipation of some major revelation.

"The scene is still so vivid in my mind," she recalls. "The three of us sat there, preparing to deal with some bombshell even as we kept checking our watches and worrying about all the other things we had to do." The man arrived 15 minutes late, sailed into the room, and announced dramatically that the way for Alison to win the debate was to wear more eye makeup than her opponent!

More than a year later, Alison can laugh easily about the encounter. But at the time, it was jarring and more than a little humiliating to a serious legislator in her third term. "I thought I'd moved beyond the stage of being judged by the color of my eyelids. But I've learned that none of us ever really does."

***

In 1995, I attended a training seminar for female officeholders sponsored by the Women's Campaign Research Fund. Dubbed "Making It to the Top," the intensive program was intended to encourage and prepare participants to do just that. For three days, national experts drilled us in campaign strategy, fundraising, speechmaking, and other essentials.

Like lipstick.

One of the skills we learned was how to apply makeup for the TV camera and for other types of public appearances (lipstick is a must, but only in shades without much blue). There were instructions about jewelry (dull-finished); necklines (high); hemlines (low); how to sit, stand, and cross our legs. Following a presentation on gestures, I overheard a woman in front of me hiss to her neighbor: "I thought this was about politics, not Emily Post!"

Indeed, political women are not infrequently surprised at the public's continuing preoccupation with how they look, sound, dress, and behave. It is an undertow that constantly churns beneath the surface of their hard-won credibility.

To be sure, political men must also be mindful of appearances, but centuries of male leadership have accustomed the electorate to many variations on a basic manly look. America's image of a female public leader, in contrast, remains a work in progress. The canvas is filled with dabs and splotches of what has been successful for others, but ultimately every woman must start from scratch with a palette of her own. The task is not trivial. Consider how the following image-related comments, all drawn from influential newspapers, erode the dignity of accomplished women:

On Hillary Clinton:
"[She looks like] a bewildered child of her changing times, sincerely trying to live up to conflicting demands."[1]
—Staff writer Susanna Moore, in the "Style" section of the *New York Times Magazine,* October 1996

On Former U. S. Representative Patricia Schroeder
"With her unctuous maternal mannerisms, [she] represents feminist sentimentality at its most saccharine."[2]
—Columnist Camille Paglia, *USA Today,* November 1996

On U. S. Senator Kay Bailey Hutchison:
"It's been called her cheerleader smile. She flashes it—there—at the television cameras. But Kay Bailey Hutchison—former cheerleader at Las Marque (Texas) High School, former cheerleader for the University of Texas Longhorns—declines to recite any of her best routines."[3]

—Staff writer Sue Ann Presley in the "Style" section of the *Washington Post,* June 1993

Every political woman must perform a high-wire image-balancing act. On the one hand, she cannot tip toward glamour or sexiness for fear of being labeled "just a pretty face" (primarily among men). On the other hand, she must keep a grip on her basic femininity, lest she appear phony or "butch" (primarily among women). It is virtually impossible to relax without tripping.

After developing and refining her public image during two successful terms in county office, Karen Martynick thought she had found solid footing, somewhere between soccer mom and professional. But it turned to quicksand when she launched a congressional campaign. "I'd give an important speech, only to have people react by saying, 'Gee, that color looks great on you!' " she recalls. "When a man gives a speech, people comment on his ideas—they don't tell him they like his suit! I learned that some people saw me as a 'looker' first and a serious candidate second; my public statements had to be twice as effective as my opponent's just to break through."

Martynick was disconcerted to find that even a veteran politician must live up to image expectations that are often unpredictable—if not unfathomable. Judge Bettieanne Hart of Augusta, Georgia was already a state legislator when she ran for the bench. Despite her experience—or perhaps because of it—she couldn't help being surprised when, after public forums on judicial issues, "of all things, people were always commenting about my hair!"

Such experiences don't necessarily mean that women's opinions or public records are being trivialized. But they do suggest that, in many races, women must still survive a visual qualifying heat before they are really in the running. Often, the performance standard is not only irrelevant but downright silly. One woman described a city council contest this way: "Both the man and the woman in the race were equally qualified, but I think that a lot of people just didn't like the woman and wanted an excuse to vote against her. You know what they came up with? Her ugly shoes!"

American women are not the only ones bemused by advice and expectations that seem to come straight from political satire. In a 1997 booklet produced by Canada's Liberal Party, female candidates were not only reminded that "your wardrobe is a reflection of you"; they were also admonished to "be prepared for mood swings." Reporters' queries on the subject of mood swings put at least one female member of parliament in the absurd position of needing to insist that "PMS is not an issue in this campaign."[4]

When it comes to matters of style, a female politician's harshest critics are frequently not her male opponents but other women. Pride in their own feminine image may be expressed as disapproval of hers. "Even before female voters allow political women to discuss specific issues, they will judge them on the basis of appearance and demeanor," wrote 1990 New York state senate candidate Sherrye Henry.[5] Commissioner Sandra Miller of Bucks County, Pennsylvania put it differently: "The reason we're so hard on each other is that we're the ones who create and share all these taboos." She suggested that "things like dangly earrings or clunky bracelets" are like a code, decipherable only to other women but deadly effective in communicating the message that this candidate is disorganized, sloppy, inattentive to detail, and, ultimately, unworthy of their votes.

Do Clothes Make the Woman?

Political women spend a good deal of time selecting clothes to show what they *aren't:* weak, unprofessional, unfocused, unworthy. Sometimes the effort is almost contortionist. Martha Wong of Houston, Texas was a grandmother when she ran for city council, but she never considered it an image issue—especially since her opponent was one, too. (It probably helped that her state's former governor had also been identified frequently by her maternal status: just after the 1990 elections, Ann Richards was summed up in the *Washington Post* as "a 57-year-old white-haired grandmother...[who beat] a West Texas oil man."[6]) That all changed when Wong heard a voter dismiss the other candidate with these words: "I could never support her—she looks like a grandmother." Realizing that she had the same vulnerabilities, Wong decided that being a grandmother was fine—as long as she looked like something else. "I always made a point of dressing in clothes that made me look strong: business suits in red and other bold, bright colors. I did the opposite of my opponent, who wore old-fashioned dresses. By the end, she had smartened up and started wearing suits, too, but hers were in pale pastels so they didn't work as well....I think that competence is not assumed in a woman candidate, and she has to use dress as a way of bolstering it."

If Wong used her style of dress to prove her mettle, Councilwoman Viola Baskerville of Richmond, Virginia relied on it to convey sensitivity and connectedness. In her socioeconomically diverse district, she took pains to appear "together, but not too bourgeois." An African-American attorney with few role models in Richmond politics, she had to find ways to look dignified without wearing stockings and high heels, or carrying a pocketbook; her outfits showed seriousness of purpose but without looking "removed from the neighborhoods." While many other women mentioned red as the color of choice for female politicians, Baskerville prefers purple—it is a play on her first name but perhaps also a statement about her ability to relate to polarized constituencies through compromise.

On a more mundane level, several officeholders commented that the sheer cost of outfitting oneself for the campaign trail may keep some women away from it. For a professional, already accustomed to business wear and attuned to fashion, there is little problem. But what of nurses, child care workers, homemakers, and others in traditionally female, often uniformed occupations? I heard this description of a female mayoral candidate from a sympathetic legislator:

> She had never worked outside the home before running for office, but she was a natural on the stump—a much better speaker, much more informed about local issues than any of her opponents. Unfortunately, she just didn't have the money to go out and buy an elaborate wardrobe. I got so angry when I'd overhear disparaging comments about her clothes: one joke among the local reporters was that she must be supportive of pawn shops because it looked like she got all her shoes from them. I'll bet that male candidates don't have people counting how many different suits they own....[I]t's just another double standard that costs us extra money on top of extra grief.

It can also cause plain physical discomfort. More than one woman told me she'd finally rebelled against aching feet and switched to tennis shoes for door-to-door campaigning, marching in parades, and the like—only to be criticized or even ridiculed for it. One legislator squeezed back into pumps after concluding that "my feet were attracting more attention than my voting record."

As suggested by Alison's experience, makeup can be tricky, too. The key for political women is to approach it not as a mask but as a window into their character and intentions. Eye makeup is most important, I was told, because it enhances the impact of visual contact, a primary means for women to communicate empathy, honesty, and interest. In fact, studies have shown that women with poor eye contact are judged incompetent, while men are simply seen as shy.[7] Skillful use of cosmetics also signals professionalism in general. For this reason, Judy Knudson began wearing makeup for the first time in her life after she became the first and only female member of the governing body in James City County, Virginia. "I was very aware that everyone was watching me," she recalls, and makeup helped establish the personal dignity and sense of decorum she wished to convey.

Speaking Their Minds—Loudly

To noted psychologist Carol Gilligan, women's voices mirror the totality of their experience. "As we have listened for centuries to the voices of men and the theories of development that their experience informs," she writes, "so we have come more recently to notice not only the silence of women but the difficulty in hearing what they say when they speak."[8] For women in politics, this is not an abstract issue.

Politicians of both genders are judged by what they say, but women especially must also mind how they say it. In particular, they are told that a soft voice connotes weakness and indecision, no matter how tough the words it delivers. In response, some women force themselves to speak much more loudly than is natural or comfortable for them; one legislator complained that her exertions leave her hoarse and addicted to lozenges and hot tea. "It's not because I can't get a microphone when I speak to an audience," she explained, "but because everyone expects me to sound like an Army drill sergeant."

The military metaphor is not accidental. Political success is constantly equated with battlefield performance, its language replete with references to war and weaponry. In a debate, the objective is to "draw blood"; opponents "fire barrages" at each other; an effective point becomes "a knock-out punch" or (even better) "a death blow." In a widely read 1996 essay about how women can improve their electability, conservative commentator Camille Paglia reinforced these norms by exhorting aspiring female politicians to spend more time studying the history of warfare and developing "military bearing"[9]—this, she argued, is the only way to make themselves acceptable to men. The assumption that women cannot lead the country because they lack military demeanor or language has a long history; early opponents of women's rights claimed that "the transfer of power from the military to the unmilitary sex involves national emasculation."[10]

Martial allusions aside, some scholars believe that the denigration of women's speech begins while they are still playing with Barbie dolls. In 1992, the American Association of University Women released a study indicating that girls speak less frequently in class than boys, are less likely to be called on by teachers, and are more often reprimanded for being impolite.[11] Communications expert Kathleen Hall Jamieson observes that "girls benefit from same-sex education in part because their voice is the norm."[12] In politics, it most assuredly is not.

Even consumer culture constantly reminds women that a voice of authority is supposed to be deep, strong, and male. Until the mid-1980's, television commercials featured female spokespersons only for products like lipstick, baby food, disinfectant, and brooms. By the end of the decade, there were women in business attire and laboratory uniforms, pitching "serious" products (like credit cards) as well as frivolous ones. But until very recently, voice-overs—the unseen announcers who function as founts of knowledge and usually close the sale—were overwhelmingly men. Even when a woman's voice was heard alone, it was usually directed to dogs, cats, children, or other women (especially dieters).[13] Is it any wonder that female politicians hear their own voices as inadequate?

There is a stark, objective measure of just how much women candidates have internalized the denigration of female voices: even the commercials of those running during the "Year of the Woman" relied almost exclusively on male voiceovers. One study of political advertising during 1992 showed that of 37 TV spots with off-camera announcers, only 6 used women—and 4 of those were commercials for a man![14]

"We need to articulate things forcefully, directly, never look like we're wavering. Women automatically come across as weak if they're not dynamic speakers," believes Martha Wong. Participants in the Women's Campaign Research Fund training seminars are admonished never to preface a thought with the phrase "I think" but always to state their opinions declaratively. One mayor commented (softly): "When a man speaks quietly, they call his voice 'measured'; but a woman just gets labeled 'not tough enough.' " Again, the balancing act: women can never risk sounding weak, but it is equally damaging to come across as bitchy, pushy, touchy, or shrill. How to avoid either extreme? A handout from the Women's Campaign School at Yale University offers two suggestions. "Keep smiling and smiling and smiling and smiling," it says; then, "If all else fails, smile." When in doubt, Georgia State Representative Kathy Ashe applies a simple rule: "You catch more flies with honey than a fly swatter."

There is also a sense that, no matter how forcefully or loudly a woman speaks, her opinions on certain subjects are likely to be ignored or dismissed—unless they are clearly more authoritative and better articulated than anyone else's. When Anita Hummer won a council seat in Elizabeth City, North Carolina, she was very conscious of people's assumption that "women aren't as knowledgeable about zoning and finance issues." Determined to prove them wrong, Hummer set herself a daunting task: she took home 11 years' worth of council meeting minutes and pored over them until she was more conversant with the city's recent evolution than anyone else. Similarly, Commissioner Karen Miller of Boone County, Missouri believes that women have little credibility on topics like roads and sewers unless they make a point of developing and showcasing expertise in those areas. "Both the press and the public are very skeptical about what you know," observes Miller. "The suspicion is: How could she be comfortable with such macho things?" Commissioner Ellie Dumdi of Lane County, Oregon perceives a bias in how she is evaluated by the press. "They use a gendered criterion in evaluating what it means to be a leader. I'm compared unfavorably to the men because

I spend my time on nitty-gritty community work; they're used to politicians who throw out a lot of grand ideas to get attention but don't necessarily follow through on them."

Dumdi specifically mentioned that the editors of the major newspaper in her area, the Eugene *Register-Guard,* were all men. However, in a weird echo of their concerns about political women failing to support each other, some officeholders complained that their harshest treatment in the press has been by female reporters. "I guess I set myself up for disappointment," said one mayor. "But I really believed that a woman who knew what it was like to function in the male-dominated journalism world would be sympathetic to one who was dealing with the same situation in politics. Was I wrong!" Another recalled her horror when a female editorial writer accused her of neglecting her teenaged children in order to get ahead. In the book *Women Politicians and the Media,* author Maria Braden traces such problems to the career pressures faced by women journalists: "Women journalists...may feel they have to prove that they are as 'tough' as their male colleagues and compensate for any suspected sympathy toward female politicians by being even tougher on them."[15]

The problem may go deeper. Perhaps, several officeholders suggested, what they're really up against is the fact that women's priorities and perspective on government, when different from men's, have generally been marginalized. For example, Kathy Ashe has made a point during her years in the Georgia legislature of specializing in banking and other traditionally "male" issues because she believes that her best chance to call attention to her talents is "to show the guys that I can be successful in dealing with problems they haven't been able to solve."

There is a silver lining. National issues—and/or widespread angst around a problem traditionally associated with home, hearth, and motherhood—can influence the winning priorities in a political career or campaign. Thus did the Anita Hill sexual harassment controversy of 1991 lead to a perception that more women were needed on Capitol Hill in 1992. The 1996 election of Jeanne Shaheen as New Hampshire's first female governor was widely credited to her emphasis on such matters as kindergarten education at precisely the time when New Hampshire parents were wringing their hands over it. As the *New York Times* reported: "Ms. Shaheen fought through a strong tradition of male and Republican domination in New Hampshire by campaigning on popular issues....[S]he focused on education issues, like financing statewide kindergarten, and home issues, like lowering the state's electric rates, which are the highest in the nation."[16]

That said, the prevailing view is that women's voices still get drowned out more selectively as well as more frequently than men's.

"Do Not Cry. Ever."

These were the words of wisdom Dianne Feinstein, then mayor of San Francisco, chose to dispense to readers of *Working Woman* magazine in 1986. She continued, "If you've got to bite off your tongue or close your eyes so tight that nobody can see what's in them, do it. Because a man can cry and somehow it doesn't bother anybody. If a woman cries, it's an immediate, destructive thing that goes out and that everybody seems to remember."[17]

"Are Female Tears Saltier Than Male Tears?" asked a *New York Times* headline the day after Representative Patricia Schroeder announced—during a tearful public speech to supporters—that she would end her 1987 quest for the presidency. And it was not just one newspaper. While Schroeder had raised numerous important issues during her short-lived campaign (not to mention the question of whether America was ready to elect a woman president), she recalls that around the country "it was my tears, not my words, that got the headlines."[18]

Ten years later, Feinstein's rule is still considered sacred. Of all the taboos applied to women politicians, the ban on tears may be the most rigid. Despite what appears to be an increased openness to public displays of emotion—the 1996 presidential contest was punctuated by frantic one-upsmanship in prime-time descriptions of personal travail—crying by political women can still be counted on to provoke horrified gasps.

At least among the women themselves. There is little concrete evidence of what voters really think but also no sense that any sort of proof is needed to establish that tears are the kiss of political death. Even during the "Year of the Woman," *Campaigns and Elections* magazine (often cited as the bible of political operatives) warned female candidates to avoid this sign of weakness.[19] Several of the women I interviewed recalled how U. S. Senator Carol Moseley-Braun had been lashed with criticism for crying when the media relentlessly questioned her about her mother's finances. "Cry today, gone tomorrow," as one mayor put it.

It is hard to imagine a serious public-affairs magazine running an article about *male* politicians titled "The Crying Game"—and yet that headline about a *woman* politician appeared in *The New Republic* in May 1996. In a lengthy critique of former U. S. Representative Enid Greene Waldholtz, the author suggested that Waldholtz purposely shed tears in public to win sympathy and divert attention from accusations of fraud and impropriety in her campaign finances. "It's condescending, not compassionate, to hold women to a different standard of culpability at the first show of tears," wrote Hanna Rosin. "So toughen up ladies, and put those handkerchiefs away."[20] Is this enlightened political commentary or proof that a woman's display of emotion will forever be more suspect than a man's?

No one I asked would admit to having cried, or knowing anyone who did, in a political setting. But I was able to gauge their feelings on the subject by showing them the following excerpt from a *New York Times Magazine* profile of two candidates in a 1996 Wisconsin congressional race. Of the female candidate, author Jeffrey Goldberg wrote: "When I comment on the nastiness of the race, she begins to cry. 'When you say that you're expecting both of us to be nasty, that's so contrary to who I am,' she says, wiping away tears."[21] Near-unanimous reaction: vigorous head-shaking, followed by comments divided equally between faulting the candidate ("She should have walked out, gone to the ladies' room, anything to avoid breaking down") and accusing Goldberg of sexism ("I'll bet he goaded her into it").

Paranoia? Insecurity? A realistic appraisal of the limits on acceptable female behavior? Or perhaps these are all answers to the wrong question. After all, the issue is only partly whether women politicians are unfairly penalized for crying. Surely it is important to ask what sorts of experiences are driving them, literally or figuratively, to tears.

Mud and Blood: Should Women Give As Good As They Get?

For at least the last decade, no national election has been complete without its ritual—and almost completely ineffective—condemnation of negative campaigning. As if on cue, professors and pundits can be counted on to lament the effects of mudslinging on an increasingly apathetic electorate. With equal predictability, politicians will shake their heads, shrug their shoulders, and blame the other guy.

Or gal. While some women officeholders try to minimize confrontation as they go about the public's business (as discussed in Chapter 5), there is no evidence that they do—or can—as candidates. For better or worse, virtually all of the women I interviewed had come to accept mud and blood as the coins of the realm of campaigning. If the female candidates of an earlier era were protected by the tradition of male chivalry (or a fear that society would condemn a man who attacked a woman), that is no longer the case—especially since a significant number of challengers, especially on the local level, are now female, too. The question is no longer whether, as women, they will be attacked—but how, as women, they can respond without causing voter backlash.

Yet again, women perceive a double standard. They do not dispute that men and women are equally vulnerable to negative campaigning; indeed, it has been clear since 1992, when both female and male U. S. Senate candidates employed the same percentage of negative TV commercials (30%), that women are approaching men in their willingness to go on the attack.[22] But at least among women who have run for lower offices, there is a strong perception that female candidates risk being punished by the electorate if they use weapons that raise nary an eyebrow when wielded by men. As described by political advertising experts Judith Trent and Robert Friedenberg, it is "the risk of being viewed as too aggressive, shrill, vicious, nagging, and 'bitchy'—in other words, unfeminine, thus losing the advantages of being perceived as nurturant, sensitive, and warm."[23] Even as increasing numbers of women take that risk, they wonder about its long-term implications—not only for themselves but also for the next generation of female politicians.

Several women who had made liberal use of attack ads received negative, sometimes blistering, feedback. It was enough to make them question whether female candidates can continue to be competitive as races get nastier but voters remain judgmental about what women should and shouldn't do.

In her 1996 Pennsylvania congressional primary, Karen Martynick used negative mailings that, in her view, were no harsher than the ones turned against her. But she was singled out for criticism. "A lot of people came up to me to express disappointment about my negative materials. It was very much on their minds. When I pointed out that my leading opponent—a man—had gone negative, too, the response was: 'We expect that of him, but not of you.' "

To Georgia Representative Kathy Ashe, "going negative" is problematic for women because they may be condemned not only for what they say but "also for seeming shrill and unsmiling when they say it." Illinois Representative Gwenn Klingler would agree. Having been challenged by a female opponent, she believes the public will turn against a woman who "comes across as a shrew," even—or especially—in comparison to another woman.

The tide may be turning. According to some recent evidence, negative political advertising has become so pervasive and formulaic that voters barely notice the gender of the candidate it is intended to promote.[24] Instead, they respond generically: A pox on both your houses. This is good news for some female candidates, who will feel freer to deploy the harsh attacks that researchers claim are more memorable and persuasive than alternative messages. But it may be bad news for women in general.

Universally and often emotionally, women around the country decry the ugly, degrading nature of campaigns, which only seems to worsen with every election. This aspect of modern politics is likely to deter potential candidates of both genders. But it is bound to disproportionately depress the number of new entrants from currently underrepresented groups because they have found other ways to express their opinions or influence their communities, thank you very much.

Councilwoman Betty Ann Krahnke of Montgomery County, Maryland sees this effect on her own three daughters. She reports with some chagrin that, despite having a successful role model right at home, none of them is interested in politics. At least in part, Krahnke believes they are reacting to an increasingly sour, vitriolic political environment—and that others in their age group will follow suit. "The harsher and more negative politics gets—the more skullduggery and name calling there is—the less appealing it's going to be to the next generation of women."

She'll get no argument from Council President Jo Ann Boscia of Lakewood, Ohio. "You get criticized, ridiculed, yelled at. The political environment has become really nasty. It's a vile atmosphere in which to run *and* to serve." Boscia predicts that a growing number of young women will weigh the unpleasant realities of politics against the exciting private sector opportunities now open to them—and opt for the latter.

Indeed, Boscia's observation—which was shared by many others—provides at least part of the answer to a question posed earlier in this book. Why has the vastly increased pool of female businesspeople and professionals not been proportionately reflected in the field of candidates? Other problems notwithstanding, women who are successfully occupied in other pursuits will not even consider entering politics unless they are strongly attracted to it. At present, my interviewees suggested, many such women are repulsed. Consider the experience of Councilwoman Adele Smith, who, as the only woman on the governing body of Ogden, Utah, feels a special responsibility to seek out potential female candidates: "I have approached any number of women and asked them to run for council. They say, 'Adele, I've seen all the criticisms of you in the newspaper and I don't know how you can stand it.' They just think about what all those attacks would do to them and their families, and they simply don't believe me when I tell them that the rewards outbalance the negatives."

A related undercurrent bubbles to the surface in a nationwide survey of 1000 American women conducted on behalf of *Ladies' Home Journal* magazine in January 1996. Of those women who are most active in their communities (involved with organizations, participating in school or neighborhood activities, and so on), only 10% have ever volunteered for a political candidate or political party. And it is more than just benign neglect: a large majority of these women express a strikingly negative attitude toward politics in general.[25]

Delaware State Senator Patricia Blevins, a veteran of unsuccessful candidate recruitment efforts, concludes: "We have to change the very negative image of politicians before we'll be able to attract a lot of new women *or* men to run." This is a tall order, especially among a group of people who have never seen themselves as part of the problem—and thus feel no obligation to be part of the solution.

Of all the comments I heard about negativism in politics, Karen Miller's was perhaps the most revealing. A successful entrepreneur who bested six male opponents the first time she ran for office,

Miller struck me as an unusually upbeat woman with a relentlessly can-do outlook. Do the personal attacks bother her? As she responded, her ebullient voice suddenly turned very quiet: "Most of my family doesn't live here, so they don't feel the hurt. But if my mother had been alive when I decided to run, I can tell you that I would have thought twice about it."

"People Will Assume You Couldn't Get a Babysitter"

As discussed in Chapter 2, the number of female candidates is also restricted by a "mommy track" mentality that can discourage mothers of school-age children from even testing the political waters. Some, however, are brave enough to jump right in. How do they stay afloat?

Almost without exception, they set rules—and stick to them. Often the rules are internal. Like any other mother, a politician with children knows when she must refuse a speaking invitation to supervise a birthday party or attend a class play. Such choices may be fraught with anxiety, but at least she learns to make them and live with them.

For Mayor Susan Bass Levin of Cherry Hill, New Jersey, the rules are explicitly laid out for her staff and constituents:

> My staff knows that when someone wants to meet with me at 5:30, they say no—because that's the time when I go home to have dinner with my family. You're the one who has to say no, that my kid is in the school play and I need to be there at 3:00. A lot of women are afraid to say that at first, but it's okay—the world doesn't come to an end!

A folk wisdom has grown up among women about how to handle the presence of young children during a campaign. Most agree that while children need not be hidden, there is no advantage to calling attention to them either. Why risk stirring up trouble, when some number of voters (or other politicians) will probably disapprove?

At least when the candidate is their mother. As Senator Blevins relates, this is not necessarily true for a father:

> I was doing campaign training for new candidates with a male colleague of mine. His advice was, "If you have young children, I urge you to bring them along. When I go out knocking on doors, I often bring my elementary school-age daughter. She charms people, and I think I pick up votes." Then it was my turn. I said, "It's different if you're a woman. Don't bring young kids when you campaign because people will just assume you couldn't get a babysitter."

This double standard for parental behavior is not just a local phenomenon. During the Senate judiciary hearings on Zoe Baird's ill-fated nomination as U. S. attorney general, she was quizzed by Senator Joseph Biden, chairman of the Judiciary Committee, about how much time she spent away from her child: what time did she leave home in the morning, and when did she return? Asked *New York Times* columnist Anthony Lewis: "Would he have asked that of any male nominee, for any job?"[26]

***

The unspoken rules of appearance, behavior, and political etiquette vary in importance and flexibility. For example, clothes worried more women than makeup; the determination to come across as emotionally impassive outweighed concerns about going on the attack. There were regional differences, too: in general, women in the South expressed greater sensitivity to dress and deportment than their counterparts elsewhere.

But everywhere, one condition was the same. Women are now free to enter politics—but they remain shackled by traditional assumptions and expectations of how they should look, act, and even feel once they get there.

8
Not Just Another Yes Man*: Where Do We Go from Here?

Ultimately, of course, the fate of political women in the next century will be decided at the ballot box. Since the majority of voters are female, it is necessary to pose a question that has always been sensitive for advocates of gender parity: should women be expected to vote for women primarily on the basis of sex?

In the 1960's and 1970's, there was good reason for answering "yes": female candidates were so rare that demonstrating their viability was a critical goal in itself. Even as recently as the mid-1980's, there were still so few women in some statehouses and in federal office that almost any female perspective could be construed as preferable to none.

Today the issue is less one of viability than of critical mass. A few female candidates have finally broken through at even the highest levels. But to fully reach their potential as partners in a democratic government—and to test their long-term effectiveness as agents of change—women must win elections in numbers that count. What role should women voters play in securing these numbers? In 1990, *New York Times* columnist William Safire saw it this way: "All other things on issues being roughly equal, women should strongly support women as women until some parity is reached. Then, secure in a system in balance, they can throw the rascals out regardless of sex."[1]

Implicit in this argument is the recognition that women politicians will not always be more deserving of women's votes than their male opponents. With the passage of time and the maturation of the women's political movement have come women candidates at extreme ends of the ideological spectrum, who by definition alienate

---

*the tag line in a campaign commercial used by Arizona U. S. Senate candidate Claire Sargent, 1992.

149

many female—and male—voters in between. In addition, women have now mounted their fair share of campaigns notable less for their principles than for mudslinging and personal attacks. When a U. S. congresswoman (Enid Greene Waldholtz) was forced out of public life in 1995 amidst financial and personal scandal, it burst whatever was left of the idealistic bubble that helped unite earlier advocates for women in the belief that theirs was a crusade for more high-minded politics.

But if some female candidates and officeholders have proven to be rascals, the vast majority have not. On the contrary, study after study has buttressed the findings of this book: that wherever they serve and whatever their personal or party beliefs, most women contribute (sometimes unconsciously) a difference in perspective that greatly enriches public service and political debate. It is not only the female members of Congress who have championed causes that particularly affect women. It is also mayors like Mickii Carter, fighting to improve local facilities for battered wives; councilwomen like Lisa Are, demanding the removal of child care responsibilities as a barrier to officeholding; and legislators like Mary Kay Budak, translating a mother's concerns into public policy that benefits everyone. As incongruous or quaint as it might sound at the end of the twentieth century, there really is such a thing as a "woman's touch" in representative government. Unfortunately, as amply demonstrated by the first-hand accounts in this book, the very life experiences that shape a woman's unique outlook can prevent her from advancing far enough in politics to make the most of it.

However, while women in office may share some common perspectives, they do not share common prescriptions for public policy. Women voters will not—and should not—overlook this when they are asked to consider a female candidate. It makes no more sense to expect all female voters to support all female politicians than it does to ask all women to *be* politicians.

Still, women politicians lose more than men when they are consigned to conventional categories like "liberal" or "conservative." Simplistic, timeworn labels do all politicians a disservice, but they are especially damaging to women who, by definition, are breaking new ground. For example, former Texas governor Ann Richards is usually lumped together with all other "liberals." But her 1990 campaign ads featured the candidate dressed in camouflage, toting a rifle, and clearly supportive of a citizen's (particularly a woman's) right to bear arms—a typical "conservative" position. When Republican Kay Bailey Hutchison ran for the U. S. Senate, her "conservative" credentials fueled bitter opposition by feminist leaders, who labeled her a "female impersonator" and warned that she was oblivious—if not actively hostile—to women's concerns. But once elected, Hutchison became a leading champion of legislation to permit individual retirement accounts for homemakers—a "woman's issue" if ever there was one.

Observers of the bitterly partisan 103rd Congress never expected its seven women senators to cross party lines—for anything. But then, in the spring of 1994, the issue of sexual harassment in the Navy came to the Senate floor. As part of the fallout from the Tailhook scandal, when naval aviators assaulted women and engaged in public sex at a Las Vegas convention, it had come time to reprimand Admiral Frank Kelso, the highest ranking officer involved in the affair. Television cameras whirred as all the women stood together, united in their demand that Kelso receive the most severe possible punishment. (It is worth noting that they were outvoted by their male colleagues, on both sides of the aisle.) More recently, attempts in Congress to roll back gender integration in the military have met with strongly bipartisan opposition among the women on Capitol Hill. In general, when the chips are down, women politicians of both parties will stand up to be counted in support of fundamental rights and opportunities for their gender.

It is demeaning to the intelligence and independence of any group of voters to dismiss the individual policy concerns of its members. At the same time, it is increasingly clear that the interests of America's women, in all their rich diversity, will best be served when there are enough female officeholders to represent that diversity. Many in public life already know this: at her confirmation hearings, Supreme Court Justice Ruth Bader Ginsburg told the Judiciary Committee that she looks forward to seeing "three, four, perhaps even more women on the high court bench, women not shaped from the same mold, but of different complexions."[2]

To that end, it is reasonable to ask each woman voter to give a female candidate a second look, an extra chance, whenever she can: that is, whenever the candidate's issue profile is at least minimally acceptable to her. When she draws up the balance sheet for a particular candidate, a woman voter is in the best position to appreciate the politically undervalued assets so often a part of women's portfolios:

nurturing or caregiving experience, occupational breadth, and sensitivity to conflicting societal roles and expectations.

***

Women politicians, for their part, are uniquely positioned to benefit from female voters' vastly increased visibility and clout. It is time for female politicians to get to know their "sisters" better: in strategic terms, to focus anew on women's concerns and on building coalitions within the female electorate.

Why now?

Of necessity, women who entered politics in the last 20 years focused much of their energy simply on getting past the door of institutions designed and controlled by men. To do so, most tried to play by the rules and internalize the norms that they had no part in shaping. These pioneering female politicians had plenty of company. Many women in the corporate world, too, aped male working styles—even their business attire—in order to get ahead.

But in the 1990's, with new skills and a keener sense of direction, more and more women are seeking their own roads. Exiting large corporations in droves, female entrepreneurs are fueling a small business explosion. Similarly, women politicians are taking chances both strategically and ideologically, forcing their colleagues to reevaluate old saws. For example, Washington Democrat Patty Murray was warned by political insiders that a self-identified "mom in tennis shoes" had no chance to win a statewide race. But her critics were left in the dust as those shoes carried her all the way into the U. S. Senate. In New Jersey, Republican Governor Christine Todd Whitman continually confounds many party leaders by combining the hard-line fiscal stance of a "conservative" with advocacy for abortion rights more rock-solid than that of many "liberals."

After the "Year of the Woman," some predicted that women's unique fundraising networks had served their purpose and would now fade into gender-neutral obscurity. Instead, the number of these groups has ballooned by 35% since 1992.[3]

Just as women politicians are coming into their own, the female electorate—long the sleeping giant of American politics—has awakened. As discussed in Chapter 4, millions more women than men register to vote, and a higher proportion of female voters has gone to the polls in every national election since 1986. Women's votes gave the leading edge to at least 25 U. S. Senate and gubernatorial candidates during the same period.[4] In 1996, for the first time in history, women determined the results of a presidential contest.

As shown in the table below, Bob Dole won a razor-thin victory among men, but Bill Clinton overcame it with a whopping 16% advantage among women. This gender gap persisted across racial lines, with 89% of black women voting for Clinton compared to 78% of black men, and even across parties: more Republican women than Republican men deserted the G.O.P. nominee, while Democratic women were the most united bloc behind Clinton.

The gender gap affects not just candidate preferences but issue priorities as well. For better or worse, the split between men's and women's votes has widened and deepened since it was first identified in the early 1980's. Attributed at first to polarizing but transitory issues like the Equal Rights Amendment, the schism has proved far more persistent and wide-ranging than early analysts ever imagined. Today, women pull the levers to assert distinctive policy concerns that are potent enough—and unifying enough—to drive elections well into the future.

Table 8.1. 1996 Presidential Election
Percent of Votes by Gender

	Clinton	*Dole*	*Perot*
All Women	54	38	7
All Men	43	44	10
Black Women	89	8	2
Black Men	78	15	5
Republican Women	15	79	5
Republican Men	11	86	6
Democratic Women	85	9	4
Democratic Men	82	11	6

Source: "The Vote Under a Microscope," Voter News Service poll of 16,627 voters. Copyright 1996 by The New York Times Co. Reprinted by permission.

A 1996 *Wall Street Journal*/NBC News poll traced the contours of this chasm. When men and women voters were asked what issue they considered most important, both chose the economy and jobs. But there the similarity ended. Nearly 40% of women perceived health care or education as a key issue, compared to 26% of men. Only one in nine women focused on the budget deficit, while one in five men did. The percentage of men who focused on taxes (12%) was twice that of women (6%). On abortion, women were more polarized.[5] And so on.

The divisions are deep as well as broad. For example, the economy seems to be, at first glance, a gender-neutral issue. But beneath the surface, women see economic ills through the lens of their own experience. Because they are more likely than men to be part-time, low-paid workers, they tend to feel more economically vulnerable and are more likely to favor a societal safety net. This is why, analysts suggest, the Dole campaign theme of economic self-reliance ("It's your money! It's your money!") fell flat among so many women; a significant percentage of women voters appear to seek a sense of security from government, not independence from it. On the other hand, the Clinton campaign effectively tapped into women's concerns with its emphasis on social security, Medicare, the minimum wage, family leave, and a host of related issues.[6]

Women were long dismissed as a special interest group with little influence or interest in the general polity. Unfortunately, large numbers have internalized this outsider status. In a 1996 survey of 1000 American women, 90% reported that they are politically uninvolved. Nearly 70% feel negative toward politics and elections, and few believe that political activity can really make a difference.[7]

The irony is that women now have the power to control the very electoral process that makes them feel so powerless. As columnist Michael Tackett wrote in the *Chicago Tribune* soon after the 1996 election: "Some 76 years after winning the right to vote, women enter the last years of the twentieth century as arguably the most important force in American politics....They have the numbers. [In public policy] the concerns of women have vaulted far ahead of those of men." But he also added: "There is a clear distinction between the power of the ballot and the power of holding office....The tension between having power and having real authority will be one of the defining battles of where women sit at the national table."[8]

This raises the issue of strategy.

There is enormous upside potential to a new focus on female voters, based on their attitudes toward government as well as on their numbers. According to a 1996 study by the Center for Policy Alternatives, a plurality of American women, but not men, believe that government has the potential to solve problems. A plurality of men, but not women, believe that government *is* the problem.[9]

The first challenge, for politicians of both genders and both parties, is to stop viewing the "women's vote" as monolithic. So-called feminist issues like abortion, sex discrimination, and affirmative action are clearly not the only ones that resonate—positively or negatively—with the female electorate. And yet, countless campaigns on every level still address women on only these issues (if they address women at all). Worse, the effort often seems a formulaic, superficial afterthought.

Even 1992 was marked by the tendency to oversimplify the "women's vote." The hyperbole that swirled around the "Year of the Woman" created an impression that virtually *all* female candidates won, swept into office on a tide of women's votes that swamped all other forces. In fact, the vast majority of female winners were those who were nominated *in districts generally favorable to their parties.*[10] Most of them were Democrats.

Across the country, more women identify as Democrats than Republicans, and female voters are usually more inclined to support the Democratic candidate in statewide races. This inclination is especially pronounced when the Democratic candidate is a woman.[11]

But gender affinity, like other human behaviors, is changeable and can shift in the winds of political evolution. For example, 1990 was a disappointing year for most female candidates. But among 1990 races that were tracked by exit polls, when the majority of women voted for the Republican, in 3 out of 4 cases that Republican was a woman.[12] In 1996, there were 6 U. S. Senate races where female and male voters made different choices, and in all of them the majority of women favored the Democrat. But the Republican who came closest to winning among women was Susan Collins of Maine.[13]

Neither party, and no individual politician, can afford to ignore women, oversimplify their concerns, or write off significant portions of the female electorate as "too liberal," "too conservative," "too divided," "too distracted"—indeed, for any reason at all. In the future, the candidate who wins the female vote will be the one (female or male) who not only takes notice of women's concerns but who actively ferrets them out.

Both female and male politicians can discern the needs of diverse groups of women and respond to those needs in accordance with their own ideologies. But a man cannot speak in a woman's voice. By virtue of biology, history, and life experience, every woman in politics has a special opportunity: to build a coalition of female voters with different opinions and priorities but a common yearning for empathy.

In business, this strategy is called "differentiated marketing." A company identifies a particular group of consumers—say, women—and develops products to satisfy as many of those consumers as possible. For instance, a magazine publisher might tailor different periodicals to college women, single working women, homemakers, working mothers, and female retirees. Across the age and lifestyle spectrum, that publisher would command more loyalty among female magazine readers and greater understanding of their needs than any competitor.

Of course, politics and public policy are very different from magazines. But the idea is similar. A woman politician should strive to inspire female voters' trust and confidence across socioeconomic groups and issue orientations. Instead of camouflaging her female identity—or insisting that it is irrelevant—she can transform it into a positive asset, a natural bridge that links her to the single largest bloc of the electorate.

And there is no reason to assume that this approach will alienate men. After all, most male voters do not reject female candidates solely on the basis of sex; why should men turn away from a set of policy concerns just because they originate with women? The strategy of coalition-building within the female electorate does not use gender as a rallying cry, and does not promote divisiveness. Rather, it acknowledges, and builds on, a stark electoral reality: that on many critical issues, the gender-neutral ground long sought by women politicians simply does not exist. Pretending otherwise not only accomplishes little; it may actually be counterproductive, by draining much of the passion that drives people into the voting booth in the first place.

***

Moreover, it is important to recognize that men have a stake in gender parity, too. Political institutions which remain highly unbalanced are breeding grounds for gender-based suspicion; both women and men seem to circle each other warily on sensitive issues, waiting for an opportunity to pounce.

Toward the end of my research for this book, newscasters and pundits around the country were abuzz with legislative proposals related to breast cancer: increasing the availability of mammograms, regulating insurance coverage for mastectomies, allocating more funds for research, and so on. What struck me about all this activity around a cancer that is virtually unique to women was the absence of a parallel burst of interest in any of the diseases unique to men; prostate cancer, in particular, kills about the same number of Americans each year as breast cancer does.

I posed this question to some legislators: why do you think that none of the men—*or* the women—in your legislature are focusing on prostate cancer? A few telling answers: "The guys just wouldn't want to put up with all the charges about sexism—who could blame them?" "I think a lot of the men feel they have to prove themselves on 'women's issues'—there's not the same pressure on 'men's issues.'" "A woman who stepped forward on that issue would be seen as pandering." "If I did it, people would say it was a publicity stunt." Such perceptions drip with discomfort that is unhealthy for everyone.

On a positive note, there are men who believe simply that women should get a shot at finding solutions to vexing social problems that have historically eluded men. One of these is George Dean, founder of a bipartisan organization called "50/50 by 2000" and a tireless promoter of women in public office throughout the country. Retired after 32 years as an advertising executive, this Harvard MBA sports few feminist credentials. He readily admits that throughout most of his life he had no interest in the obstacles facing women. Nevertheless, after watching female officials in action, Dean became convinced—and set out to convince others—that women can find new ways to tackle old issues like health, education, and child welfare.[14]

More women mean a larger candidate pool for both parties— and more choices for voters of both genders. While George Dean is exceptional in the national scope of his activities, there are clearly growing numbers of lower-profile, politically active men who recognize the value of boosting their female counterparts.

***

It is simple logic: because the vast majority of incumbents at all levels of elective office are men, any limit on their tenure will open up opportunities for women and other underrepresented groups. This dimension is generally overlooked by most term limit proponents, who talk a good deal about out-of-touch career politicians but very little about the types of people who might replace them.

The outlook for federally imposed term limits is dim. In early 1997, a proposed constitutional amendment was defeated in the House of Representatives by 69 votes—not only well below the two-thirds majority required for constitutional amendments but 10 votes fewer than the tally in favor of a term limits proposal two years earlier.

But hope lingers at other levels of government. Ballot referenda directing legislators to address this issue have passed in almost half the states, often by impressive margins, and have been defeated in only seven. Term limitation sentiment has also been strongly expressed in some major cities, such as Houston and New York.

The major argument against term limits is that they underestimate—in fact, pointedly reject—the value of political experience. But millions of voters have now weighed in on the issue: they agree that in a representative democracy, experience may be good but fresh perspectives and diverse opinions are better. Indeed, early experience with legislative term limits in California and Maine has been promising—and notably feminizing.

Despite continuing legal challenges to term limits in California, the number of women in the state assembly has jumped by 25%. Almost half of the body's 27 committees were led by women during 1997. The reason is obvious to Assemblywoman Carole Migden, chair of the powerful Appropriations Committee: "Most people don't get Appropriations in six years...but I got it in six months. Who says term limits isn't working?"[15]

In Maine, even the *Wall Street Journal,* hardly a bastion of feminist journalism, was struck by the gender transformation. "As part of increased turnover—40% of legislators are freshmen—Maine now has its first female House speaker," the *Journal* reported, "and half of the legislature's leaders are women, the most ever."[16] The title of the article rendered the newspaper's overall judgment: "As Term Limits Take Effect in Maine's Capitol, Government Seems to Be Doing Just Fine, Thanks."

***

For the most part, the story of women in politics in the 1990's is less about roadblocks than speed bumps. This is very good news. It is finally possible for women—at least, for some of them—to run campaigns, snare victories, and build records of achievement that are every bit the equal of men's.

But speed bumps can still be formidable; while they may not keep women out of the process, their bone-jarring effects certainly make it hard to keep women in. This book has attempted to uncover and describe these remaining impediments—the first step toward dislodging them.

With these speed bumps out of the way, the road will be clear. But where does it lead? What should be the ultimate goal? It should not be a reprise of "The Year of the Woman," which after all limited women's impact to a span of only 365 days. As we enter a new century, the goal should be considerably more ambitious: to foster full and equal partnerships between women and men; to value individuality and diversity; and to ensure that all citizens feel a vital part of the political process.

Appendix:
Women's PAC's and Donor Networks

The following list includes 57 political action committees and donor networks that either give money predominantly to women candidates or have a predominantly female donor base. It does not include state affiliates of national organizations or issue PACs without a gender identification.

The organizations are grouped according to the geographic scope of their activity: 12 operate nationally, and 45 are state-based. The national organizations devote some resources to women running for state legislatures, but they are largely focused on developing and supporting candidates for federal offices and for governorships. The state-based groups commonly train and/or support local as well as state-level candidates. Some of these organizations support only the candidates of one party, and/or candidates with a stipulated position on abortion rights. Where relevant and verifiable, these criteria are indicated as follows:

Democratic only - DEM

Republican only - REP

Pro-choice only - PC

Pro-life only - PL

The author wishes to thank the Center for the American Woman and Politics, part of the Eagleton Institute of Politics at Rutgers University, for permission to reprint this list. While it represents the best information available in 1997, users should keep in mind that some of these organizations, especially on the state level, may change, move, or become inactive over time.

National Organizations

American Nurses' Association, Inc. (ANA-PAC)
Contact: Kathleen Shumacher, PAC Coordinator
600 Maryland Ave. SW, Suite 100W
Washington, DC 20024-2571
(202) 651-7095
FAX: (202) 554-0189

EMILY's List
Contact: Mary Beth Cahill, Executive Director
Ellen Malcolm, President
805 15th St., Suite 400
Washington, DC 20005
(202) 326-1400
FAX: (202) 326-1415
DEM, PC

National Federation of Business and Professional Women's Clubs (BPW/PAC)
Contact: Mariwyn Heath, BPW/PAC Chair
2012 Massachusetts Ave., NW
Washington, DC 20036
(202) 293-1100, ext. 555

National Organization for Women PAC
Contact: Linda Berg, Political Director
1000 16th St., NW, Suite 700
Washington, DC 20036-5705
(202) 331-0066
FAX: (202) 785-8576
PC

National Women's Political Caucus
Contact: Heather Herndon, Political Director
1211 Connecticut Ave., NW, Suite 425
Washington, DC 20036
(202) 785-1100
FAX: (202) 785-3605
PC

RENEW (Republican Network To Elect Women)
Contact: Margaret Barton or Karen Roberts, Co-Presidents
1555 King St., Suite 200
P.O. Box 507
Alexandria, VA 22313-0507
(703) 836-2255
REP

The Susan B. Anthony List
Contact: Jane Abraham, President
919 Prince St.
Alexandria, VA 22313
(703) 683-5558
FAX: (703) 549-5588
PL

WISH List
Contact: Karen Raye, Executive Director
3205 N. St. NW
Washington, DC 20007
(202) 342-9111
FAX: (202) 342-9190
REP, PC

Women in Psychology for
  Legislative Action
Contact: Dr. Noreen Johnson,
  Treasurer
13 Ashfield St.
Roslindale, MA 02131
(617) 327-8015

Women's Campaign Fund
Contact: Amy Sobel, Managing
  Director
  Amy Walter, Political Director
734 15th St., NW, Suite 500
Washington, DC 20002
(202) 393-8164
FAX: (202) 544-4517
PC

Women's Council of the
  Democratic Senatorial
  Campaign Committee
Contact: Tracy Buckman,
  Director
430 South Capitol St., SE
Washington, DC 20003
(202) 224-2447
FAX: (202) 485-3120
DEM

Women's Pro-Israel National
  PAC (WIN PAC)
Contact: Jane Glaser
2020 Pennsylvania Ave., NW
Washington, DC 20006
(202) 296-2946

State-Based Organizations

Alabama
Alabama Solution
Contact: Cameron Vowell,
  Treasurer
  Bernadette Chapman,
  Executive Secretary
P.O. Box 370821
Birmingham, AL 35237
(205) 250-0205
FAX: (205) 995-1990

Focus 2020
Contact: Cindy Paler
P.O. Box 660
Huntsville, AL 35804-0660

Arkansas
Arkansas Women's Action Fund
Contact: Sherry Mather,
  President
  Mary Dillard, Former President
1100 North University, Suite 109
Little Rock, AR 72707
(501) 663-1202
FAX: (501) 663-1218
PC

California
Democratic Activists for Women
  Now (DAWN)
P.O. Box 6614
San Jose, CA 95150
DEM, PC

Eleanor Roosevelt Fund of California
Contact: Andrea Leiderman
1001-158 Evelyn Terrace East
Sunnyvale, CA 94086
(408) 773-9791

HOPE-PAC
Contact: Maria Contreras-Sweet, President
3220 E 26th St.
Los Angeles, CA 90023
(213) 267-5845
FAX: (213) 262-1348

Latina PAC
Contact: Dina Hidalgo, Co-Chair
915 L St., Suite C, #222
Sacramento, CA 95814
(916) 395-7915

Los Angeles African American Women's PAC
Contact: Celestine Palmer, Chair
4102 Olympiad Dr.
Los Angeles, CA 90043
(213) 295-2382

Los Angeles Women's Campaign Fund
Contact: Barbara Rosenbaum, Treasurer
c/o Kreff and Rosenbaum
1410 Ventura Blvd., Suite 402
Sherman Oaks, CA 91423
(818) 990-7377
FAX: (818) 990-1840

Marin County Women's PAC
Contact: Johanna Willmann, Chair
3310 Paradise Dr.
Tiburon, CA 94920
(415) 435-2504

Sacramento Women's Campaign Fund
Contact: Toni Roberts, Chair
P.O. Box 162212
Sacramento, CA 95816
(916) 443-8421
FAX: (916) 443-8440
PC

Santa Barbara Women's Political Committee
Contact: Hannah Beth Jackson or Susan Rose
P.O. Box 90618
Santa Barbara, CA 93190-0618
(805) 682-6769
PC

Wednesday Committee
Contact: Adrianna Babior, Facilitator
1531 Purdue
Los Angeles, CA 90025
(310) 477-8081
Note: The Wednesday Committee is not a PAC but a network of PACs in the Los Angeles area.

Women For:
Contact: Lucie Bava,
 Coordinator
8913 West Olympic Blvd., Suite 103
Beverly Hills, CA 90211-3552
(310) 657-7411
FAX: (310) 289-0719
PC

Women for Orange County
Contact: Shirley Palley,
 President
P.O. Box 5402
Irvine, CA 92716
(714) 854-8024
PC

Women's Political Committee
Contact: Syd Whalley or Stacy
 Phillips, Co-Chairs
5670 Wilshire Blvd., #1450
Los Angeles, CA 90036
(310) 558-8114
FAX: (310) 558-8309
PC

Women's Political Fund
Contact: D. J. Soviero
P.O. Box 421811
San Francisco, CA 94142-1811
(415) 861-5168
PC

Women's Political Summit
Contact: Adrianna Babior
1531 Purdue
Los Angeles, CA 90025
(310) 477-8081
Note: The Women's Political Summit is not a PAC but a network of PACs in California.

Connecticut
Women Organizing Women PAC (WOW PAC)
Contact: Sue Faris, Treasurer
233 Everit
New Haven, CT 06511

Delaware
PAC of the Women's Democratic Club of Delaware
Contact: Kathy Jamison,
 President
402 West Clearview Ave.
Wilmington, DE 19809
(302) 798-2028
FAX: (302) 798-3153
DEM, PC

Women's Democratic Club of Delaware
Contact: Kathy Jamison,
 President
(302) 798-2028
FAX: (302) 798-3153
E-mail: wdcofde@aol.com
DEM, PC

Florida
GWEN's List
Contact: Karen Gievers,
 President
4410 Flagler St.
Miami Beach, FL 33130
(305) 374-0521
DEM

Indiana
Indiana Women's Network for Political Action
Contact: Dr. Carolyn Cooke or Dr. Elyche Howard, Co-Chairs
P.O. Box 88271
Indianapolis, IN 46208-0271
(317) 283-2066
PC

Kentucky
EMMA's List
P.O. Box 64
Louisville, KY 40201-0646

Louisiana
Committee of 21
Contact: Brenda Hatfield, President
P.O. Box 19287
New Orleans, LA 70179
(504) 827-0112

Independent Women's Organization
Contact: Angelique Reed, President
13834 Octvia St.
New Orleans, LA 70125
(504) 525-2256

Maryland
Harriet's List
Contact: Sayra Wells Meyerhoff, Chair
P.O. Box 16361
Baltimore, MD 21210
(410) 377-5709
FAX: (410) 377-2842
DEM, PC

Michigan
Michigan Women's Campaign Fund
Contact: Nina Abrams, Chair
P.O. Box 71626
Madison Heights, MI 48071
(810) 932-3540
FAX: (810) 932-1734
PC

Minnesota
Minnesota Women's Campaign Fund
Contact: Mary Martin, Administrator
550 Rice St., Suite 106
St. Paul, MN 55103
(612) 904-6723
FAX: (612) 292-9417
PC

Missouri
Missouri Women's Action Fund
Contact: Vivian Eveloff, First Vice-Chair
1108 Hillside Dr.
St. Louis, MO 63117
(314) 516-6622

New Jersey
GROW (Greater Roles and Opportunities for Women, Inc.)
Contact: Kayla Bergeron, Executive Director
29 Emmons Dr.
Building F, Suite 4
Princeton, NJ 08540
(609) 989-7300
REP

PAM's List
P.O. Box 3311
Cherry Hill, NJ 08034
DEM, PC

Republican Women of the 90's
Contact: Lynn Shapiro,
  Executive Director
2 Hartford Dr.
Tinton Falls, NJ 07724
(732) 530-8927
REP

Women's Political Action
  Committee of NJ
Contact: Patricia Connolly,
  President
P.O. Box 170
Edison, NJ 08818
(908) 638-6784

New York
The Women's TAP Fund (Taking
  Action in Politics)
Contact: Jane Griffin
64 Tudor Place
Buffalo, NY 14222
(716) 881-3241
PC

Ohio
The Hope Chest
Contact: Pat Larson, Steering
  Committee Chair
4921 Dierker Rd.
Columbus, OH 43220
(614) 236-4268
FAX: (614) 236-2449
DEM, PC

Oklahoma
First Ladies of Oklahoma
Contact: Vickie Cleveland, First
  Vice-President
8364 S Urbana Ave.
Tulsa, OK 74137
REP

Voices of Oklahoma Women
  (VOW)
Contact: Elizabeth Stoll Hager
6002 S Atlanta Court
Tulsa, OK 74105
(405) 749-5629

Oregon
Women's Investment Network
  (WIN-PAC)
Contact: Jewel Lansing
3333 SW Arnold
Portland, OR 97219
(503) 246-6022
DEM, PC

Pennsylvania
Ain't I A Woman Network/PAC
Contact: Cynthia Moultrie
P.O. Box 34484
Philadelphia, PA 19101

Pennsylvania Women's
  Campaign Fund
Contact: Nancy Neuman
P.O. Box 767
Hazleton, PA 18201

Tennessee
Women in the Nineties (WIN)
Contact: Elliott McNeil, Chief
 Staff Officer
1215 Seventh Ave. N
P.O. Box 50452
Nashville, TN 37208
(615) 298-1250
FAX: (615) 298-9858

Texas
Task Force 2000 PAC
Contact: Jeanette Di Filippo
P.O. Box 36183
Houston, TX 77236
(281) 495-7539
FAX: (281) 495-0594

Virginia
The Leader PAC
Contact: Sally Atwater, Chair
P.O. Box 7001
Fairfax Station, VA 22039-7001

Make Women Count
Contact: Laurie Janus,
 Administrative Director
P.O. Box 677
Richmond, VA 23218-0677
(804) 644-7450
FAX: (804) 643-1466

Notes

Introduction
1. Denise Baer, "Political Parties: The Missing Variable in Women and Politics Research," *Political Research Quarterly,* vol. 46 (Sept. 1993), p. 555.
2. Adrienne Rich, *On Lies, Secrets and Silence* (New York: W. W. Norton, 1979), p. 214.

Chapter 1
1. Fact Sheet, National Information Bank on Women in Public Office, Center for the American Woman and Politics, Eagleton Institute of Politics, Rutgers University (July 1995).
2. R. Darcy and Sarah Slavin Schramm, "When Women Run Against Men," *Public Opinion Quarterly,* vol. 41 (Spring 1977), pp. 1-12.
3. Susan Carroll, "The Political Careers of Women Elected Officials: An Assessment and Research Agenda," in Shirley Williams and Edward L. Lascher, Jr., *Ambition and Beyond: Career Paths of American Politicians* (Berkeley, CA: University of California Institute of Government Studies, 1993), p. 205; Nancy E. McGlen and Karen O'Connor, *Women, Politics and American Society* (Englewood Cliffs, NJ: Prentice-Hall, 1995), p. 62.
4. *Voices, Views, Votes: Women in the 103rd Congress* (Research report of the Center for the American Woman and Politics, Eagleton Institute of Politics, Rutgers University, 1995); also see Karen Foerstel and Herbert Foerstel, *Climbing the Hill: Gender Conflict in Congress* (Westport, CT: Praeger, 1996), pp. 127-40.
5. *The Impact of Women in Public Office: An Overview* (Research report of the Center for the American Woman and Politics, Eagleton Institute of Politics, Rutgers University, 1991).
6. Fact Sheet, National Information Bank on Women in Public Office, Center for the American Woman and Politics, Eagleton Institute of Politics, Rutgers University (Spring 1997).

7. "Reapportionment, Redistricting and Women: The Dangers and Opportunities in California," *News and Notes,* Center for the American Woman and Politics, Eagleton Institute of Politics, Rutgers University, vol. 7, no. 1 (1989), pp. 14-15.
8. R. Darcy, Susan Welch and Janet Clark, *Women, Elections and Representation* (Lincoln, NE: University of Nebraska Press, 1994), pp. 74-75; Clyde Wilcox, "Why Was 1992 the 'Year of the Woman'? Explaining Women's Gains in 1992," in Elizabeth Cook, Sue Thomas and Clyde Wilcox, eds., *The Year of the Woman: Myths and Realities* (Boulder, CO: Westview Press, 1994), pp. 17-18.
9. Center for the American Woman and Politics, Eagleton Institute of Politics, Rutgers University (Telephone query, Dec. 1996).
10. Tony Perry, "Whatever Happened to the 'Year of the Woman'?" *Los Angeles Times,* Nov. 20, 1995, p. 1.
11. "Compensation and Benefits for State Legislators" (Research report of the National Conference of State Legislatures, March 28, 1995); Sam Howe Verhovek, "State Lawmakers Prepare to Wield Vast New Powers," *New York Times,* Sept. 4, 1995, p. A1.
12. Beth Donovan, "Women's Campaigns Fueled Mostly by Women's Checks," *Congressional Quarterly Weekly Report,* vol. 50, no. 41 (1992), pp. 3269-73.
13. As examples, see Barbara Burrell, "Women's and Men's Campaigns for the U.S. House of Representatives, 1972-1982: A Finance Gap?" *American Politics Quarterly,* vol. 13 (1985), pp. 251-72; Carole Uhlaner and Kay Schlozman, "Candidate Gender and Congressional Campaign Receipts," *Journal of Politics,* vol. 48 (July 1986), pp. 30-50.
14. Carole Chaney and Barbara Sinclair, "Women and the 1992 House Elections," in Cook, Thomas and Wilcox, p. 128.
15. Darcy, Welch and Clark, p. 79.
16. Ibid., pp. 65-67.
17. Cindy Simon Rosenthal, "Once They Get There: The Role of Gender in Legislative Careers," *Extensions: Journal of the Carl Albert Congressional Research and Studies Center* (Spring 1995), p. 16.
18. Cited in Alan McConagha, "Inside Politics," *Washington Times,* Dec. 16, 1994, p. A5.
19. Christine B. Williams, "Women, Law and Politics: Recruitment Patterns in the Fifty States," *Women and Politics,* vol. 10, no. 3 (1990), p. 104.
20. Wendy Kaminer, "Crashing the Locker Room," *Atlantic Monthly* (July 1992), p. 60.

21. Quoted in Maria Braden, *Women Politicians and the Media* (Lexington, KY: University of Kentucky Press, 1996), p. 120.
22. Darcy, Welch and Clark, p. 126.
23. Fact Sheets, National Information Bank on Women in Public Office, Center for the American Woman and Politics, Eagleton Institute of Politics, Rutgers University (October 1992 and July 1995).
24. "Women Make News as Voters, Edge Upward as Candidates," *News and Notes,* Center for the American Woman and Politics, Eagleton Institute of Politics, Rutgers University, vol. 11, no. 2 (Spring 1997), p. 1.
25. Richard S. Dunham and Susan B. Garland, "The Year of the Woman—Really," *Business Week,* Oct. 26, 1992, p. 106.
26. Glenna Matthews, "Women Candidates in the 1990's: Behind the Numbers," *Extensions: Journal of the Carl Albert Congressional Research and Studies Center* (Spring 1995), p. 4.
27. Susan Carroll, *Women as Candidates in American Politics* (Bloomington, IN: Indiana University Press, 1994), pp. 38-45.
28. Timothy Bledsoe and Mary Herring, "Victims of Circumstances: Women in Pursuit of Political Office," *American Political Science Review,* vol. 84, no. 1 (1990), pp. 217-18, 221; Edmond Constantini, "Political Women and Political Ambition: Closing the Gender Gap," *American Journal of Political Science,* vol. 34, no. 3 (1990), pp. 749-55.
29. Laura Van Assendelft and Karen O'Connor, "Backgrounds, Motivations and Interests: A Comparison of Male and Female Local Party Activists," *Women and Politics,* vol. 14, no. 3 (1994), p. 85; Constantini, p. 754.
30. Bledsoe and Herring, p. 218.
31. As an example, see Ann Morrison, Randall White and Ellen Van Velson, *Breaking the Glass Ceiling* (New York: Addison-Wesley, 1992).
32. Judith Dobrzynski, "Study Finds Few Women in 5 Highest Company Jobs*," New York Times,* Oct. 18, 1996, p. D4.
33. Joan Jeruchim and Pat Shapiro, *Women, Mentors and Success* (New York: Fawcett Columbine, 1992); also see Belle Rose Ragins and Terri A. Scandura, "Gender Differences in Expected Outcomes of Mentoring Relationships," *Academy of Management Journal,* vol. 37, no. 4 (1994), pp. 957-71; K. E. Kram, *Mentoring at Work* (Glenview, IL: Scott, Foresman, 1985); R. J. Burke and C. A. McKeen, "Mentoring in Organizations: Implications for Women," *Journal of Business Ethics,* vol. 9 (1990), pp. 317-32.
34. Andrew Harris, "Break the Glass Ceiling for Senior Executives," *HR Focus* (March 1994), p. 4; also see Carol T. Schreiber, Karl F. Price and Ann Morrison, "Workforce Diversity and the Glass Ceiling: Practices,

Barriers, Possibilities," *Human Resource Planning,* vol. 16, no. 2 (1993), pp. 51-69.
35. Eleanor Petersen, "Retrospective Commentaries on Two Women, Three Men in a Raft," *Harvard Business Review,* vol. 72 (May/June 1994), p. 80.
36. Cited in Judith Dobrzynski, "Gaps and Barriers, and Women's Careers," *New York Times,* Feb. 28, 1996, p. D2.
37. Quoted in Karen Dewitt, "Job Bias Cited for Minorities and Women: The Glass Ceiling Is Real, Panel Says," *New York Times,* Nov. 23, 1995, p. A21.
38. Quoted in Jennifer Laabs, "The Sticky Floor Beneath the Glass Ceiling," *Personnel Journal,* vol. 72 (May 1993), pp. 35-39.
39. Barbara J. Nelson and Najma Chowdhury, "Redefining Politics: Patterns of Women's Political Engagement from a Global Perspective," in Barbara J. Nelson and Najma Chowdhury, eds., *Women and Politics Worldwide* (New Haven, CT: Yale University Press, 1994), p. 3.
40. Elizabeth Vallance, "Where the Power Is, Women Are Not," *Parliamentary Affairs,* vol. 35 (Spring 1982), pp. 218-19.

Chapter 2

1. Carol Nechemias, "Geographic Mobility and Women's Access to State Legislatures," *Western Political Quarterly,* vol. 38 (March 1985), p. 127; Susan J. Carroll and Wendy S. Strimling, *Women's Routes to Elective Office: A Comparison With Men's,* Center for the American Woman and Politics, Eagleton Institute of Politics, Rutgers University (1983), pp. 28-29.
2. Quoted in Jennifer Warren, "It's a Vote Against Motherhood, Says Rebuffed Candidate," *Los Angeles Times,* April 8, 1994, p. 3A.
3. Quoted in Karen Foerstel and Herbert Foerstel, *Climbing the Hill: Gender Conflict in Congress* (Westport, CT: Praeger, 1996), p. 116.
4. Melinda Henneberger, "Preaching Moderation on Her Own Side of the Aisle," *New York Times,* July 20, 1997, N.J. Section, p. 2.
5. Quoted in Michael D'Antonio, "If I'd Only Known Then What I Know Now," *Redbook* (Sept. 1996), p. 100.
6. Quoted in Marjorie Margolies-Mezvinsky, *A Woman's Place: The Freshmen Women Who Changed the Face of Congress* (New York: Crown Publishers, 1994), p. 174.
7. Rose Mary Wentling, "Women in Middle Management: Their Career Development and Aspirations," *Business Horizons,* vol. 35 (Jan/Feb 1992), p. 48.

8. Sharon A. Lobel and Lynda St. Clair, "Effects of Family Responsibilities, Gender and Career Identity Salience on Performance Outcomes," *Academy of Management Journal,* vol. 35, no. 5 (1992), p. 1066.
9. Phyllis Tharenou, Shane Latimer and Denise Conroy, "How Do You Make It to the Top? An Examination of Influences on Women's and Men's Managerial Advancement," *Academy of Management Journal,* vol. 37, no. 4 (1994), p. 925.
10. Marcia Manning Lee, "Why Few Women Hold Public Office: Democracy and Sexual Roles," *Political Science Quarterly,* vol. 31, no. 2 (1976), p. 306.
11. Quoted in Richard S. Dunham and Susan B. Garland, "The Year of the Woman—Really," *Business Week,* Oct. 26, 1992, p. 106.
12. Quoted in John E. Yang, "Political Parent Trap II," *Washington Post,* June 30, 1996, p. A8.
13. As an example, see Sue Shellenbarger, "Shedding Light on Women's Records Dispels Stereotypes," *Wall Street Journal,* Dec. 30, 1995, p. A15.
14. Susan J. Carroll, "The Personal Is Political: The Intersection of Private Lives and Public Roles Among Women and Men in Elective and Appointive Office," *Women and Politics,* vol. 9, no. 2 (1989), p. 61.
15. Terri Apter, *Working Women Don't Have Wives* (New York: St. Martin's Press, 1993), p. 22.
16. Susan Gluck Mezey, "Increasing the Number of Women in Office: Does It Matter?" in Elizabeth Cook, Sue Thomas and Clyde Wilcox, eds., *The Year of the Woman: Myths and Realities* (Boulder, CO: Westview Press, 1994), p. 257.
17. Carroll and Strimling, pp. 32-40.
18. Patricia Freeman and William Lyons, "Female Legislators: Is There a New Type of Woman in Office?" in Gary Moncrief and Joel A. Thompson, eds., *Changing Patterns in State Legislative Careers* (Ann Arbor, MI: University of Michigan Press, 1992), p. 65.
19. Carroll and Strimling, p. 51.
20. Susan J. Carroll, *Women as Candidates in American Politics* (Bloomington, IN: Indiana University Press, 1994), pp. 130-31.

Chapter 3

1. William Safire, "Bad Year For Women," *New York Times,* Dec. 20, 1990, p. A31.
2. Women's Campaign Fund promotional literature, 1995.
3. National Women's Political Caucus promotional literature, 1996.

4. Candace J. Nelson, "Women's PACs in the Year of the Woman," in Elizabeth Cook, Sue Thomas and Clyde Wilcox, eds., *The Year of the Woman: Myths and Realities* (Boulder, CO: Westview Press, 1994), p. 187-91.
5. Make Women Count promotional literature, 1996.
6. Daniel J. Brass, "Men's and Women's Networks: A Study of Interaction Patterns and Influence in an Organization," *Academy of Management Journal,* vol. 28, no. 2 (1985), pp. 339-41.
7. Rosabeth M. Kanter, *Men and Women of the Corporation* (New York: Basic Books, 1977), pp. 208-9.
8. Joan Jeruchim and Pat Shapiro, *Women, Mentors and Success* (New York: Fawcett Columbine, 1992), p. 54; also see Kathy Kram, "Phases of the Mentor Relationship," *Academy of Management Journal,* vol. 26, no. 4 (1983), pp. 608-25; Phyllis Tharenou, Shane Latimer and Denise Conroy, "How Do You Make It to the Top? An Examination of Influences on Women's and Men's Managerial Advancement," *Academy of Management Journal,* vol. 37, no.4 (1994), pp. 899-931; Belle Rose Ragins and John Cotton, "Easier Said Than Done: Gender Differences in Perceived Barriers to Gaining a Mentor," *Academy of Management Journal,* vol. 34 (1991), pp. 939-51.
9. Jeruchim and Shapiro, p. 66.
10. Susan Crandell, "The Joys (and Payoffs) of Mentoring," *Executive Female* (March/April 1994), p. 38.
11. Ibid., p. 40.
12. "Work Week," *Wall Street Journal,* June 10, 1997, p. A1.
13. Jeruchim and Shapiro, p. 60.
14. Ibid., p. 61.
15. Quoted in Art Weissman, "Women's Progress Lags," *Asbury Park Press,* Dec. 3, 1996, p. A1.
16. Patricia Schroeder, "To the New Women in Congress: Here's How to Survive," *Glamour* (Feb. 1997), p. 96.
17. Terri Apter, *Working Women Don't Have Wives* (New York: St. Martin's Press, 1993), p. 221.
18. "Women Candidates in 1996," *News and Notes,* Center for the American Woman and Politics, Eagleton Institute of Politics, Rutgers University, vol. 11, no. 1 (Summer 1996), pp. 14-25.
19. Elizabeth Kolbert, "Is the Tactic Teamwork or Cynicism?" *New York Times,* April 24, 1997, p. B1.
20. Quoted in Sherrye Henry, *The Deep Divide: Why American Women Resist Equality* (New York: MacMillan, 1994), p. 374.

21. Ellen Goodman, syndicated column, *Washington Post,* Sept. 12, 1992.
22. Quoted in Maria Braden, *Women Politicians and the Media* (Lexington, KY: University of Kentucky Press, 1995), p. 140.
23. Quoted in Henry, p. 374.
24. Joyce Purnick, "Metro Matters," *New York Times,* August 29, 1996, p. B3.
25. Quoted in Purnick, p. B3.
26. Nelson, p. 185.
27. Rebekah Herrick, "A Reappraisal of the Quality of Women Candidates," *Women and Politics,* vol. 15, no. 4 (1995), p. 30.
28. Ibid., p. 36.
29. Richard Berke, "Year of Woman Falters in 2 Races for Governor," *New York Times,* Nov. 1, 1993, p. B9.
30. Joseph Sullivan, "Whitman Pins Hopes on Women," *New York Times,* Oct. 31, 1993, NJ Section, p.1.
31. Geraldine Ferraro, Letter to the editor, *New York Times,* Oct. 26, 1995.
32. Cited in Braden, p. 184.
33. Sherrye Henry, "Why Women Don't Vote for Women Candidates and Why They Should," *Working Woman,* vol. 19, no. 6 (June 1994), p. 51.

Chapter 4

1. Susan Carroll, *Women as Candidates in American Politics* (Bloomington, IN: Indiana University Press, 1994), pp. 123-24.
2. Quoted in Charles G. McGuigan, "Viola O. Baskerville: North Side's City Councilwoman," *Northside Magazine,* Stone Arch Publications of Richmond, VA, vol. 2, no. 12 (Dec. 1995), p. 1.
3. Susan Carroll, "The Political Careers of Women Elected Officials: An Assessment and Research Agenda," in Shirley Williams and Edward L. Lascher, Jr., eds., *Ambition and Beyond: Career Paths of American Politicians* (Berkeley, CA: University of California Institute of Governmental Studies, 1993), p. 204.
4. "Compensation and Benefits for State Legislators" (Research report of the National Conference of State Legislatures, March 28, 1995).
5. Ibid.
6. Gary Moncrief and Joel Thompson, *Changing Patterns in State Legislative Careers* (Ann Arbor, MI: University of Michigan Press, 1992).
7. Quoted in Howie Carr, "The 10 Dumbest Pols," *Boston Magazine,* vol. 88, no. 7 (July 1996), p. 51.

8. National Conference of State Legislatures, 1995.
9. For examples, see Marilyn Loden Bilensky, *Feminine Leadership: Or How to Succeed in Business Without Being One of the Boys* (New York: Times Books, 1985); Gwen Rubenstein, "Women on the Way Up," *Association Management,* vol. 38, no. 10 (Oct. 1986), pp. 26-30; Sally Helgesen, *The Female Advantage* (New York: Doubleday, 1990).
10. Cited in Judy B. Rosener, "Ways Women Lead," *Harvard Business Review,* vol. 68 (Nov.-Dec. 1990), p. 121.
11. Rita Mae Kelly, Mary M. Hale and Jayne Burgess, "Gender and Managerial/Leadership Styles: A Comparison of Arizona Public Administrators," *Women and Politics,* vol. 11, no. 2 (1991), pp. 22-23.
12. Quoted in Liz Roman Gallese, "Why Women Aren't Making It to the Top," *Across the Board,* vol. 28 (April 1991), p. 19.
13. Edmond Constantini, "Political Women and Political Ambition: Closing the Gender Gap," *American Journal of Political Science,* vol. 34, no. 3 (August 1990), p. 759; also see Laura Van Assendelft and Karen O'Connor, "Backgrounds, Motivations and Interests: A Comparison of Male and Female Local Party Activists," *Women and Politics,* vol. 14, no. 3 (1994), p. 88.
14. Timothy Bledsoe and Mary Herring, "Victims of Circumstances: Women in Pursuit of Political Office," *American Political Science Review,* vol. 84, no.1 (March 1990), p. 218.
15. "Delegate Cheryl C. Kagan," *Guide to Maryland Legislators 1995-1998,* Bancroft Information Group, Inc., p. 412.
16. Irwin Gertzog, *Congressional Women* (Westport, CT: Praeger, 1995).
17. Quoted in Wendy Kaminer, "Crashing the Locker Room," *Atlantic Monthly* (July 1992), p. 60.
18. Quoted in Joan Jeruchim and Pat Shapiro, *Women, Mentors and Success* (New York: Fawcett Columbine, 1992), p. 57.
19. Judith H. Dobrzynski, "Gaps and Barriers, and Women's Careers," *New York Times,* Feb. 28, 1996, p. D2.
20. Herminia Ibarra, "Personal Networks of Women and Minorities in Management: A Conceptual Framework," *Academy of Management Review,* vol. 18, no. 1 (1993), pp. 56-87.
21. Susan Carroll, Debra L. Dodson and Ruth B. Mandel, *The Impact of Women in Public Office,* Center for the American Woman and Politics, Eagleton Institute of Politics, Rutgers University (1991), pp. 25-31.
22. Glenn Collins, "Unforeseen Business Barriers for Women," in Bette Ann Stead, ed., *Women in Management* (Englewood Cliffs, NJ: Prentice-Hall, 1985), pp. 161-64.

23. Anne Tsui, Terri Egan and Charles O'Reilly, III, "Being Different: Relational Demography and Organizational Attachment," *Administrative Science Quarterly,* vol. 37 (1992), pp. 549-79; Ellen A. Fagenson, "Is What's Good for the Goose Also Good for the Gander? On Being White and Male in a Diverse Workforce," *Academy of Management Executive,* vol. 7, no. 4 (1993), pp. 80-81.
24. Linda Himelstein, "Breaking Through," *Business Week,* Feb. 17, 1997, pp. 68-69.
25. "Fact Sheet: Women in State Legislatures 1995," Center for the American Woman and Politics, Eagleton Institute of Politics, Rutgers University (Nov. 1995).
26. Rose Mary Wentling, "Women in Middle Management: Their Career Development and Aspirations," *Business Horizons,* vol. 35 (Jan./Feb. 1992), p. 51.
27. Cited in Nancy McGlen and Karen O'Connor, *Women, Politics and American Society* (Englewood Cliffs, NJ: Prentice-Hall, 1995), p. 63.
28. Clyde Brown, Neil R. Heighberger and Peter A. Shocket, "Gender-Based Differences in Perceptions of Male and Female City Council Candidates," *Women and Politics,* vol. 13, no. 1 (1993), p. 8.
29. Patricia K. Freeman and William Lyons, "Legislators' Perceptions of Women in State Legislatures," *Women and Politics,* vol. 10, no. 4 (1990), p. 128.
30. Carroll, *Women As Candidates,* p. 205.
31. McGlen and O'Connor, p. 63.
32. Ellen Goodman, "What We Think Vs. What We Do," *Graduate Woman,* vol. 78, no. 5 (May 1984), p. 4.
33. Carroll, *Women As Candidates,* p. 163.
34. Sherrye Henry, *The Deep Divide: Why American Women Resist Equality* (New York: MacMillan, 1994), p. 389.

Chapter 5

1. Quoted in Dorothy Cantor and Toni Bernay, *Women in Power* (New York: Houghton Mifflin, 1992), p. 288.
2. Sandra Lipsitz Bem, "Probing the Promise of Androgyny," in Mary Roth Walsh, ed., *The Psychology of Women: Ongoing Debates* (New Haven, CT: Yale University Press, 1987), pp. 207-8.
3. Quoted in Carla Anne Robbins and Laurie McGinley, "Washington's Spotlight Starts to Follow the Women," *Wall Street Journal,* August 25, 1997, p. A20.

4. Judy B. Rosener, "Ways Women Lead," *Harvard Business Review,* vol. 68 (Nov-Dec 1990), p. 120.
5. Ibid., p. 124.
6. Carolyn Duff, *When Women Work Together* (Berkeley, CA: Conari Press, 1993), pp. 37-40, 99-103.
7. Cited in "'Work Week': Female Executives Score Well in Gender Study," *Wall Street Journal,* Sept. 24, 1996, p. Al.
8. Quoted in Karen Foerstel and Herbert N. Foerstel, *Climbing the Hill: Gender Conflict in Congress* (Westport, CT: Praeger, 1996), p. 135.
9. Ibid.
10. Susan Carroll, Debra Dodson and Ruth Mandel, *The Impact of Women in Public Office: An Overview,* Center for the American Woman and Politics, Eagleton Institute of Politics, Rutgers University (1991), pp. 22-23; Debra Dodson and Susan Carroll, *Reshaping the Agenda: Women in the State Legislatures,* Center for the American Woman and Politics, Eagleton Institute of Politics, Rutgers University (1991), p. 87.
11. Ibid.
12. John Nichols, "Georgia's Cinderella Story," *The Nation,* Nov. 11, 1996, p. 18.
13. Marilyn Johnson and Susan Carroll with Kathy Stanwyck and Lynn Korenblit, *Profile of Women Holding Office II* (Metuchen, NJ: Scarecrow Press, 1978); Jeane Kirkpatrick, *Political Woman* (New York: Basic Books, 1974).
14. R. Darcy, Susan Welch and Janet Clark, *Women, Elections and Representation* (Lincoln, NE: University of Nebraska Press, 1994), pp. 182-3.

Chapter 6

1. Edmond Constantini, "Political Women and Political Ambition: Closing the Gender Gap," *American Journal of Political Science,* vol. 34, no. 3 (1990), p. 763.
2. Denise Baer, "Political Parties: The Missing Variable in Women and Politics Research," *Political Research Quarterly,* vol. 46 (Sept 1993), p. 559.
3. Daryl Glenney, "Women in Politics: On the Rise," *Campaigns and Elections,* vol. 3 (Winter 1982), pp. 18-24.
4. Jill Abramson, "GOP's Historic Win Was Actually Plotted by Female Politicos," *Wall Street Journal,* Jan. 5, 1995, p. 1 [paraphrased with permission of Dow Jones and Co., Inc.].
5. Mary Lou Kendrigan, *Political Equality in a Democratic Society* (Westport, CT: Greenwood Press, 1984), pp. 101-2.

6. Nancy E. McGlen and Karen O'Connor, *Women, Politics and American Society* (Englewood Cliffs, NJ: Prentice Hall, 1995), p. 82.
7. Paul Lewis, "In the World's Parliaments, Women Are Still a Small Minority," *New York Times,* March 16, 1997, p. 1, On-Line Report.
8. For examples, see Laura Van Assendelft and Karen O'Connor, "Backgrounds, Motivations and Interests: A Comparison of Male and Female Local Party Activists," *Women and Politics*, vol. 14, no. 3 (1994), pp. 77-90; Constantini, pp. 741-70; Timothy Bledsoe and Mary Herring, "Victims of Circumstances: Women in Pursuit of Political Office," *American Political Science Review,* vol. 84, no. 1 (1990), pp. 213-23; Diane L. Fowlkes, Jerry Perkins and Sue Tolleson Rinehart, "Gender Roles and Party Roles," *American Political Science Review,* vol. 73 (1979), pp. 772-80.
9. Constantini, p. 763.
10. Quoted in Leslie Wayne, "Business Is Biggest Campaign Spender," *New York Times,* Oct. 18, 1996, p. A1.
11. Report of the Interagency Committee on Women's Business Enterprise and the National Women's Business Council, as cited in Stephanie Mehta, "Number of Women-Owned Businesses Surged 43% in 5 Years Through 1992," *Wall Street Journal,* Jan. 29, 1996, p. B2.
12. Baer, p. 565.
13. Van Assendelft and O'Connor, p. 86.
14. Susan J. Carroll and Wendy S. Strimling, *Women's Routes to Elective Office: A Comparison with Men's,* Center for the American Woman and Politics, Eagleton Institute of Politics, Rutgers University (1983), p. 83.
15. Susan J. Carroll, "The Political Careers of Women Elected Officials: An Assessment and Research Agenda," in Shirley Williams and Edward L. Lascher, Jr., eds., *Ambition and Beyond: Career Paths of American Politicians* (Berkeley, CA: University of California Institute of Government Studies, 1993), p. 213; Summary of data from a series of research reports entitled "Bringing More Women into Public Office," published by the Center for the American Woman and Politics, Eagleton Institute of Politics, Rutgers University (1983-1986).
16. Carroll and Strimling, pp. 84-85.

Chapter 7

1. Quoted in Susanna Moore, "The Body Politic," *New York Times Magazine,* Oct. 6, 1996, p. 73.
2. Camille Paglia, "Coddling Won't Elect Women; Toughening Will," *USA Today,* Nov. 12, 1996, p. 14A.

3. Sue Ann Presley, "Style," *Washington Post,* June 14, 1993, p. 1, Style Section.
4. "Sunday," *New York Times Magazine,* June 1, 1997, p. 23.
5. Sherrye Henry, *The Deep Divide: Why American Women Resist Equality* (New York: MacMillan, 1994), pp. 237-38.
6. Robert Suro, "The 1990 Elections: Governor - Texas; Fierce Election for Governor Is Narrowly Won By Richards," *Washington Post,* Nov. 7, 1990, p. 2.
7. Kathleen Hall Jamieson, *Beyond the Double Bind: Women and Leadership* (New York: Oxford University Press, 1995), p. 123.
8. Carol Gilligan, *In a Different Voice* (Cambridge, MA: Harvard University Press, 1982), p. 173.
9. Paglia, p. 14A.
10. Mary Putnam-Jacobi, *Common Sense Applied to Woman Suffrage* (New York: G. P. Putnam's Sons, 1894), p. 94.
11. "How Schools Shortchange Girls" (Report prepared for the American Association of University Women Education Foundation by the Wellesley College Center for Research on Women, 1992).
12. Jamieson, p. 82.
13. Lynn T. Lovdal, "Sex Role Messages in Television Commercials: An Update," *Sex Roles,* vol. 21, no. 11/12 (1989), pp. 720-21.
14. Leonard Williams, "Political Advertising in the 'Year of the Woman': Did X Mark the Spot?" in Elizabeth Cook, Sue Thomas and Clyde Wilcox, eds., *The Year of the Woman: Myths and Realities* (Boulder, CO: Westview Press, 1994), p. 202.
15. Maria Braden, *Women Politicians and the Media* (Lexington, KY: University of Kentucky Press, 1996), p. 167.
16. "The Elections," special section of the *New York Times,* Nov. 6, 1996, p. B7.
17. Quoted in Jerry Roberts, *Dianne Feinstein: Never Let Them See You Cry* (New York: HarperCollins West, 1994), p. 4.
18. Quoted in Braden, p. 192.
19. Ibid., p. 133.
20. Hanna Rosin, "The Crying Game," *The New Republic,* May 27, 1996, p. 4.
21. Jeffrey Goldberg, "Adventures of a Republican Revolutionary," *New York Times Magazine,* Nov. 3, 1996, p. 81.
22. Williams, p. 206.

23. Judith S. Trent and Robert V. Friedenberg, *Political Campaign Communication: Principles and Practices* (Westport, CT: Praeger, 1991), p. 137.
24. David Procter, William Schenck-Hamlin and Karen Haase, "Exploring the Role of Gender in the Development of Negative Political Advertisements," *Women and Politics,* vol. 14, no. 2 (1994), pp. 18-19.
25. Pamela Guthrie O'Brien, "Women Voters Fed Up and Furious," *Ladies Home Journal* (June 1996), pp. 88, 96.
26. Anthony Lewis, "If It Were Mr. Baird," *New York Times,* Jan. 25, 1993, p. A17.

Chapter 8

1. William Safire, "Bad Year For Women," *New York Times,* Dec. 20, 1990, p. A 31.
2. Quoted in Kathleen Hall Jamieson, *Beyond the Double Bind: Women and Leadership* (New York: Oxford University Press, 1995), p. 98.
3. Based on lists of women's PACs and donor networks in *News and Notes,* Center for the American Woman and Politics, Eagleton Institute of Politics, Rutgers University, vol. 8, no. 2 (Spring 1992), pp. 10-12 and in "Women's PACs and Donor Networks: A Contact List," Center for the American Woman and Politics, Eagleton Institute of Politics, Rutgers University (June 1997).
4. "Fact Sheet: The Gender Gap," Center for the American Woman and Politics, Eagleton Institute of Politics, Rutgers University (August 1994).
5. Albert R. Hunt, "Democrats' Delight: Clinton's Edge with Women Goes Far Beyond Abortion Issue," *Wall Street Journal,* Sept. 20, 1996, p. R6.
6. Debra Dodson, "Women Voters and the Gender Gap," *News and Notes,* Center for the American Woman and Politics, Eagleton Institute of Politics, Rutgers University, vol. 11, no. 2 (Spring 1997), pp. 27-32.
7. Pamela Guthrie O'Brien, "Women Voters Fed Up and Furious," *Ladies Home Journal* (June 1996), pp. 88, 96.
8. Michael Tackett, "Politicos Have Seen the Future...And It's Women," *Chicago Tribune,* Dec. 8, 1996, p. 1, Section 2.
9. "Women's Voices: Solutions for a New Economy" (Report prepared for the Center for Policy Alternatives by Lake Research, Sept. 1996), p. 3.
10. Carole Chaney and Barbara Sinclair, "Women and the 1992 House Elections," in Elizabeth Cook, Sue Thomas and Clyde Wilcox, eds., *The Year of the Woman: Myths and Realities* (Boulder, CO: Westview Press, 1994), pp. 134-35.

11. "The Gender Gap in 1996: Setting the Context," *News and Notes,* Center for the American Woman and Politics, Eagleton Institute of Politics, Rutgers University, vol. 11, no. 1 (Summer 1996), p. 2.
12. "Fact Sheet: The Gender Gap," Center for the American Woman and Politics, Eagleton Institute of Politics, Rutgers University (August 1994).
13. "Gender Gap Evident in Numerous 1996 Races," *News and Notes,* Center for the American Woman and Politics, Rutgers University, vol. 11, no. 2 (Spring 1997), p. 3.
14. George Tunick, "A Kindred Spirit," *Executive Female* (May/June 1993), p. 70.
15. Quoted in B. Drummond Ayres, Jr., "State Term Limits Are Transforming the Legislatures," *New York Times,* April 28, 1997, p. A13.
16. Dana Milbank, "As Term Limits Take Effect in Maine's Capitol, Government Seems to Be Doing Just Fine, Thanks," *Wall Street Journal,* April 2, 1997, p. A16.

Bibliography

Books

Apter, Terri. *Working Women Don't Have Wives.* New York: St. Martin's Press, 1993.

Belinsky, Marilyn Loden. *Feminine Leadership: Or How To Succeed in Business without Being One of the Boys.* New York: Times Books, 1985.

Braden, Maria. *Women Politicians and the Media.* Lexington: University of Kentucky Press, 1995.

Cantor, Dorothy and Toni Bernay. *Women in Power.* New York: Houghton Mifflin, 1992.

Carroll, Susan. *Women As Candidates in American Politics.* Bloomington: Indiana University Press, 1994.

Carroll, Susan J. and Wendy S. Strimling. *Women's Routes to Elective Office: A Comparison with Men's.* New Brunswick, NJ: Center for the American Woman and Politics, Eagleton Institute of Politics, Rutgers University, 1983.

Cook, Elizabeth, Sue Thomas and Clyde Wilcox, eds. *The Year of the Woman: Myths and Realities.* Boulder, CO: Westview Press, 1994.

Darcy, R., Susan Welch and Janet Clark. *Women, Elections and Representation.* Lincoln: University of Nebraska Press, 1994.

Dodson, Debra and Susan Carroll. *Reshaping the Agenda: Women in the State Legislatures.* New Brunswick, NJ: Center for the American Woman and Politics, Eagleton Institute of Politics, Rutgers University, 1991.

Duff, Carolyn. *When Women Work Together.* Berkeley, CA: Conari Press, 1993.

Foerstel, Karen and Herbert N. Foerstel. *Climbing the Hill: Gender Conflict in Congress.* Westport, CT: Praeger, 1996.

Gertzog, Irwin. *Congressional Women.* Westport, CT: Praeger, 1995.

Gilligan, Carol. *In a Different Voice.* Cambridge, MA: Harvard University Press, 1982.

Guide to Maryland Legislators 1995-1998. Bancroft Information Group, Inc., 1995.

Helgesen, Sally. *The Female Advantage: Women's Ways of Leadership.* New York: Doubleday, 1990.

Henry, Sherrye. *The Deep Divide: Why American Women Resist Equality.* New York: MacMillan, 1994.

Jamieson, Kathleen Hall. *Beyond the Double Bind: Women and Leadership.* New York: Oxford University Press, 1995.

Jeruchim, Joan and Pat Shapiro. *Women, Mentors and Success.* New York: Fawcett Columbine, 1992.

Johnson, Marilyn and Susan Carroll with Kathy Stanwyck and Lynn Korenblit. *Profile of Women Holding Office II.* Metuchen, NJ: Scarecrow Press, 1978.

Kanter, Rosabeth M. *Men and Women of the Corporation.* New York: Basic Books, 1977.

Kendrigan, Mary Lou. *Political Equality in a Democratic Society.* Westport, CT: Greenwood Press, 1984.

Kirkpatrick, Jeane. *Political Woman.* New York: Basic Books, 1974.

Kram, K. E. *Mentoring at Work.* Glenview, IL: Scott, Foresman, 1985.

Mandel, Ruth. *In the Running.* Boston, MA: Beacon Press, 1983.

Margolies-Mezvinsky, Marjorie. *A Woman's Place: The Freshmen Women Who Changed the Face of Congress.* New York: Crown Publishers, 1994.

McGlen, Nancy E. and Karen O'Connor. *Women, Politics and American Society.* Englewood Cliffs, NJ: Prentice-Hall, 1995.

Moncrief, Gary and Joel Thompson. *Changing Patterns in State Legislative Careers.* Ann Arbor: University of Michigan Press, 1992.

Morrison, Ann, Randall White and Ellen Van Velson. *Breaking the Glass Ceiling.* New York: Addison-Wesley, 1992.

Putnam-Jacobi, Mary. *Common Sense Applied to Woman Suffrage.* New York: Putnam's Sons, 1894.

Rich, Adrienne. *On Lies, Secrets and Silence.* New York: W. W. Norton, 1979.

Roberts, Jerry. *Dianne Feinstein: Never Let Them See You Cry.* New York: Harper Collins West, 1994.

Stead, Bette Ann, ed. *Women in Management.* Englewood Cliffs, NJ: Prentice-Hall, 1985.

Trent, Judith S. and Robert V. Friedenberg. *Political Campaign Communication: Principles and Practices.* Westport, CT: Praeger, 1991.

Walsh, Mary Roth. *The Psychology of Women: Ongoing Debates.* New Haven, CT: Yale University Press, 1987.

Williams, Shirley and Edward L. Lascher, Jr., eds. *Ambition and Beyond: Career Paths of American Politicians.* Berkeley, CA: University of California Institute of Governmental Studies, 1993.

Articles

Abramson, Jill. "GOP's Historic Win Was Actually Plotted by Female Politicos." *Wall Street Journal,* 5 January 1995, 1.

Ayres, B. Drummond, Jr. "State Term Limits Are Transforming the Legislatures." *New York Times,* 28 April 1997, 1.

Baer, Denise. "Political Parties: The Missing Variable in Women and Politics Research." *Political Research Quarterly* 46 (September 1993): 547-70.

Bem, Sandra Lipsitz. "Probing the Promise of Androgyny." In Mary Roth Walsh, ed., *The Psychology of Women: Ongoing Debates,* 206-25. New Haven, CT: Yale University Press, 1987.

Berke, Richard. "Year of Woman Falters in 2 Races for Governor." *New York Times,* 1 Nov. 1993, B9.

Bledsoe, Timothy and Mary Herring. "Victims of Circumstances: Women in Pursuit of Political Office." *American Political Science Review* 84 (1990): 213-23.

Brass, Daniel J. "Men's and Women's Networks: A Study of Interaction Patterns and Influence in an Organization." *Academy of Management Journal* 28 (1985): 327-43.

"Bringing More Women into Public Office." Center for the American Woman and Politics, Eagleton Institute of Politics, Rutgers University (1983).

Brown, Clyde, Neil R. Heighberger and Peter A. Shocket. "Gender Based Differences in Perceptions of Male and Female City Council Candidates." *Women in Politics* 13 (1993): 1-17.

Burke, R. J. and C. A. McKeen. "Mentoring in Organizations: Implications for Women." *Journal of Business Ethics* 9 (1990): 317-32.

Burrell, Barbara. "Women's and Men's Campaigns for the U.S. House of Representatives, 1972-1982: A Finance Gap?" *American Politics Quarterly* 13 (1985): 251-72.

Carr, Howie. "The 10 Dumbest Pols." *Boston Magazine* 88 (July 1996): 50.

Carroll, Susan J. "The Personal Is Political: The Intersection of Private Lives and Public Roles Among Women and Men in Elective and Appointive Office." *Women and Politics* 9 (1989): 51-65.

Carroll, Susan J. "The Political Careers of Women Elected Officials: An Assessment and Research Agenda." In Shirley Williams and Edward L. Lascher, Jr., eds., *Ambition and Beyond: Career Paths of American Politicians,* 197-230. Berkeley, CA: University of California Institute of Governmental Studies, 1993.

Chaney, Carole and Barbara Sinclair. "Women and the 1992 House Elections." In Elizabeth Cook, Sue Thomas and Clyde Wilcox, eds., *The Year of the Woman: Myths and Realities,* 123-39. Boulder, CO: Westview Press, 1994.

Collins, Glenn. "Unforeseen Business Barriers for Women." In Bette Ann Stead, ed., *Women in Management,* 161-64. Englewood Cliffs, NJ: Prentice Hall, 1985.

"Compensation and Benefits for State Legislators." Research report of the National Conference of State Legislatures, 28 March 1995.

Constantini, Edmond. "Political Women and Political Ambition: Closing the Gender Gap." *American Journal of Political Science* 34 (August 1990): 741-70.

Crandell, Susan. "The Joys (and Payoffs) of Mentoring." *Executive Female* 1 (March/April 1994): 38.

D'Antonio, Michael. "If I'd Only Known Then What I Know Now." *Redbook* (September 1996): 100.

Darcy, R., Margaret Brewer and Judy Clay. "Women in the Oklahoma Political System: State Legislative Elections." *Social Science Journal* 21 (1984): 67-78.

Darcy, R. and Sarah Slavin Schramm. "When Women Run Against Men." *Public Opinion Quarterly* 41 (Spring 1977): 1-12.

DeWitt, Karen. "Job Bias Cited for Minorities and Women: The Glass Ceiling Is Real, Panel Says." *New York Times* , 23 Nov. 1995, 21.

Dobrzynski, Judith. "Gaps and Barriers, and Women's Careers." *New York Times,* 28 Feb. 1996, D2.

Dobrzynski, Judith. "Study Finds Few Women in 5 Highest Company Jobs." *New York Times,* 18 Oct. 1996, D4.

Dodson, Debra. "Women Voters and the Gender Gap." In Center for the American Woman and Politics, Eagleton Institute of Politics, Rutgers University, *News and Notes* 11 (Spring 1997): 27-32.

Donovan, Beth. "Women's Campaigns Fueled Mostly by Women's Checks." *Congressional Quarterly Weekly Report* 50 (1992): 3269-73.

Dunham, Richard S. and Susan B. Garland. "The Year of the Woman—Really." *Business Week* (26 Oct. 1992): 106.

Duskin, Meg S. "Number of Women Office Holders Edges Upward." *The National Voter* (Dec./Jan. 1997): 11.

"The Elections." Special section of the *New York Times,* 6 Nov. 1996, B7.

Fact Sheet. "The Gender Gap." Center for the American Woman and Politics, Eagleton Institute of Politics, Rutgers University (August 1994).

Fact Sheet. National Information Bank on Women in Public Office, Center for the American Woman and Politics, Eagleton Institute of Politics, Rutgers University (August 1996).

Fact Sheet. National Information Bank on Women in Public Office, Center for the American Woman and Politics, Eagleton Institute of Politics, Rutgers University (July 1995).

Fact Sheet. "Women in State Legislatures 1995." Center for the American Woman and Politics, Eagleton Institute of Politics, Rutgers University (November 1995).

Fagenson, Ellen A. "Is What's Good for the Goose Also Good for the Gander? On Being White and Male in a Diverse Workforce." *Academy of Management Executive* 7 (1993): 80-81.

Ferraro, Geraldine. Letter to the editor, *New York Times,* 26 Oct. 1994.

Fowlkes, Diane L., Jerry Perkins and Sue Tolleson Rinehart. "Gender Roles and Party Roles." *American Political Science Review* 73 (1979): 772-80.

Freeman, Patricia K. and William Lyons. "Female Legislators: Is there a New Type of Woman in Office?" In Gary Moncrief and Joel A. Thompson, eds., *Changing Patterns in State Legislative Careers,* 59-73. Ann Arbor: University of Michigan Press, 1992.

Freeman, Patricia K. and William Lyons. "Legislators' Perceptions of Women in State Legislatures." *Women and Politics* 10 (1990): 121-32.

Gallese, Liz Roman. "Why Women Aren't Making It to the Top." *Across the Board* 28 (April 1991): 18.

"Gender Gap a Factor in a Majority of Races in 1990." In Center for the American Woman and Politics, Eagleton Institute of Politics, Rutgers University, *News and Notes* 8 (1991): 4.

"Gender Gap Evident in Numerous 1996 Races." In Center for the American Woman and Politics, Eagleton Institute of Politics, Rutgers University, *News and Notes* 11 (Spring 1997): 3.

"The Gender Gap in 1996: Setting the Context." In Center for the American Woman and Politics, Eagleton Institute of Politics, Rutgers University, *News and Notes* 11 (Summer 1996): 2.

Glenney, Daryl. "Women in Politics: On the Rise." *Campaigns and Elections* 3 (Winter 1982): 18.

Goldberg, Jeffrey. "Adventures of a Republican Revolutionary." *New York Times Magazine,* 3 Nov. 1996, 42.

Goodman, Ellen. Syndicated column. *Washington Post,* 12 September 1992.

Goodman, Ellen. "What We Think vs. What We Do." *Graduate Woman* (publication of the American Association of University Women) 78 (May 1984): 4.

Harris, Andrew. "Break the Glass Ceiling for Senior Executives." *HR Focus* (March 1994): 1.

Henry, Sherrye. "Why Women Don't Vote for Women Candidates and Why They Should." *Working Woman* 19 (June 1994): 48.

Herrick, Rebekah. "A Reappraisal of the Quality of Women Candidates." *Women and Politics* 15 (1995): 25-38.

Himelstein, Linda. "Breaking Through." *Business Week,* 17 Feb. 1997, 65.

"How Schools Shortchange Girls." Wellesley College Center for Research on Women, AAUW Educational Foundation, Washington, DC, 1992.

Hunt, Albert R. "Democrats' Delight: Clinton's Edge with Women Goes Far Beyond Abortion Issue." *Wall Street Journal,* 20 Sept 1996, R1.

Ibarra, Herminia. "Personal Networks of Women and Minorities in Management: A Conceptual Framework." *Academy of Management Review* 18 (1993): 56-87.

The Impact of Women in Public Office: An Overview. Research report of the Center for the American Woman and Politics, Eagleton Institute of Politics, Rutgers University (1991).

Kaminer, Wendy. "Crashing the Locker Room." *Atlantic Monthly* (July 1992): 60.

Kelly, Rita Mae, Mary M. Hale and Jayne Burgess. "Gender and Managerial/Leadership Styles: A Comparison of Arizona Public Administrators." *Women and Politics* 11 (1991): 19-39.

Kolbert, Elizabeth. "Is the Tactic Teamwork or Cynicism?" *New York Times,* 24 April 1997, B1.

Kram, Kathy. "Phases of the Mentor Relationship." *Academy of Management Journal* 26 (1983): 608-25.

Laabs, Jennifer. "The Sticky Floor Beneath the Glass Ceiling." *Personnel Journal* 72 (May 1993): 35-39.

Lee, Marcia Manning. "Why Few Women Hold Public Office: Democracy and Sexual Roles." *Political Science Quarterly* 31 (1976): 306.

Lewis, Anthony. "If It Were Mr. Baird." *New York Times,* 25 Jan. 1993, A17.

Lewis, Paul. "In the World's Parliaments, Women Are Still a Small Minority." *New York Times,* 16 March 1997, On-line report.

Lobel, Sharon A. and Lynda St. Clair. "Effects of Family Responsibilities, Gender and Career Identity Salience on Performance Outcomes." *Academy of Management Journal* 35 (1992): 1057-69.

Lovdal, Lynn T. "Sex Role Messages in Television Commercials: An Update." *Sex Roles* 21 (1989): 715-24.

Make Women Count promotional literature (1996).

Matthews, Glenna. "Women Candidates in the 1990's: Behind the Numbers." *Extensions: Journal of the Carl Albert Congressional Research and Studies Center* (Spring 1995): 3-6.

McConagha, Alan. "Inside Politics." *Washington Times*, 16 Dec. 1994, A5.

McGuigan, Charles G. "Viola O. Baskerville: North Side's City Councilwoman." *Northside Magazine* (Richmond, VA: Stone Arch Publications) 2 (Dec. 1995): 1.

Mehta, Stephanie. "Number of Women-Owned Businesses Surged 43% in 5 Years Through 1992." *Wall Street Journal*, 29 Jan. 1996, B2.

Mezey, Susan Gluck. "Increasing the Number of Women in Office: Does It Matter?" In Elizabeth Cook, Sue Thomas and Clyde Wilcox, eds., *The Year of the Woman: Myths and Realities*, 257-70. Boulder, CO: Westview Press (1994).

Milbank, Dana. "As Term Limits Take Effect in Maine's Capitol, Government Seems To Be Doing Just Fine, Thanks." *Wall Street Journal*, 2 April 1997, A16.

Mills, Kay. *Los Angeles Times*, 10 Nov. 1990, B7.

Moore, Susanna. "The Body Politic." *New York Times Magazine*, 6 Oct. 1996, 73.

National Women's Political Caucus promotional literature (1996).

Nechemias, Carol. "Geographic Mobility and Women's Access to State Legislatures." *Western Political Quarterly* 38 (March 1985): 119-31.

Nelson, Barbara J. and Najma Chowdhury. "Redefining Politics: Patterns of Women's Political Engagement from a Global Perspective." In Barbara Nelson and Najma Chowdhury, eds., *Women and Politics Worldwide*, 3. New Haven, CT: Yale University Press, 1994.

Nelson, Candice J. "Women's PACs in the Year of the Woman." In Elizabeth Cook, Sue Thomas and Clyde Wilcox, eds., *The Year of the Woman: Myths and Realities*, 181-96. Boulder, CO: Westview Press, 1994.

Nichols, John. "Georgia's Cinderella Story." *The Nation*, 11 Nov. 1996, 18.

O'Brien, Pamela Guthrie. "Women Voters Fed Up and Furious." *Ladies Home Journal* (June 1996): 88.

Paglia, Camille. "Coddling Won't Elect Women; Toughening Will." *USA Today,* 12 Nov. 1996, A14.

Perry, Tony. "Remember 'The Year of the Woman'?" *Los Angeles Times,* 23 Nov. 1995.

Perry, Tony. "Whatever Happened to the 'Year of the Woman'?" *Los Angeles Times,* 20 Nov. 1995, 1.

Petersen, Eleanor. "Retrospective Commentaries on Two Women, Three Men on a Raft." *Harvard Business Review* 72 (May/June 1994): 68-71.

Presley, Sue Ann. "Style." *Washington Post,* Style Section,14 June 1993, 1.

Proctor, David, William Schenck-Hamlin and Karen Haase. "Exploring the Role of Gender in the Development of Negative Political Advertisements." *Women and Politics* 14 (1994): 1-22.

Purnick, Joyce. "Metro Matters." *New York Times,* 29 August 1996, B3.

Ragins, Belle Rose and John Cotton. "Easier Said Than Done: Gender Differences in Perceived Barriers to Gaining a Mentor." *Academy of Management Journal* 34 (1991): 939-51.

"Reapportionment, Redistricting and Women: The Dangers and Opportunities in California." In Center for the American Woman and Politics, Eagleton Institute of Politics, Rutgers University, *News and Notes* 7 (1989): 14-15.

Robbins, Carla Anne and Laurie McGinley. "Washington's Spotlight Starts to Follow the Women." *Wall Street Journal,* 25 August 1997, A20.

Rosener, Judy B. "Ways Women Lead." *Harvard Business Review* 68 (Nov.-Dec. 1990): 119-25.

Rosenthal, Cindy Simon. "Once They Get There: The Role of Gender in Legislative Careers." *Extensions: Journal of the Carl Albert Congressional Research and Studies Center* (Spring 1995): 15-17.

Rosin, Hanna. "The Crying Game." *The New Republic,* 27 May 1996, 4.

Rubenstein, Gwen. "Women on the Way Up." *Association Management* 38 (Oct. 1986): 26-30.

Safire, William. "Bad Year for Women." *New York Times,* 20 Dec. 1990, A31.

Schreiber, Carol T., Karl F. Price and Ann Morrison. "Workforce Diversity and the Glass Ceiling: Practices, Barriers, Possibilities." *Human Resource Planning* 16 (1993): 51-69.

Schroeder, Patricia. "To the New Women in Congress: Here's How to Survive." *Glamour* (Feb. 1997): 96.

Shellenbarger, Sue. "Shedding Light on Women's Records Dispels Stereotypes." *Wall Street Journal,* 30 Dec. 1995, 15.

Sullivan, Joseph. "Whitman Pins Hopes on Women." *New York Times,* NJ Section, 31 Oct. 1993, 1.

Suro, Robert. "The 1990 Elections: Governor-Texas; Fierce Election for Governor Is Narrowly Won by Richards." *Washington Post,* 7 Nov. 1990, 2.

Tackett, Michael. "Politicos Have Seen the Future...And It's Women." *Chicago Tribune,* Section 2, 8 Dec. 1996, 1.

Tharenou, Phyllis, Shane Latimer and Denise Conroy. "How Do You Make It to the Top? An Examination of Influences on Women's and Men's Managerial Advancement." *Academy of Management Journal* 37 (1994): 899-931.

Tsui, Anne, Terri Egan and Charles O'Reilly, III. "Being Different: Relational Demography and Organizational Attachment." *Administrative Science Quarterly* 37 (1992): 549-79.

Tunick, George. "A Kindred Spirit." *Executive Female* (May/June 1993): 70.

Uhlaner, Carole and Kay Schlozman. "Candidate Gender and Congressional Campaign Receipts." *Journal of Politics* 48 (July 1986): 30-50.

Vallance, Elizabeth. "Where the Power Is, Women Are Not." *Parliamentary Affairs* 35 (Spring 1982): 218-19.

Van Assendelft, Laura and Karen O'Connor. "Backgrounds, Motivations, and Interests: A Comparison of Male and Female Local Party Activists." *Women and Politics* 14 (1994): 77-92.

Verhovek, Sam Howe. "State Lawmakers Prepare to Wield Vast New Powers." *New York Times,* 4 Sept. 1995, 1.

Voices, Views, Votes: Women in the 103rd Congress. Research report of the Center for the American Woman and Politics, Eagleton Institute of Politics, Rutgers University (1995).

Warren, Jennifer. "It's a Vote Against Motherhood, Says Rebuffed Candidate." *Los Angeles Times,* 8 April 1994, 3A.

Wayne, Leslie. "Business Is Biggest Campaign Spender." *New York Times,* 18 Oct. 1996, 1.

Weissman, Art. "Women's Progress Lags." *Asbury Park Press,* 3 Dec. 1996, A1.

Wentling, Rose Mary. "Women in Middle Management: Their Career Development and Aspirations." *Business Horizons* 35 (Jan/Feb 1992): 47-54.

Williams, Christine B. "Women, Law and Politics: Recruitment Patterns in the Fifty States." *Women and Politics* 10 (1990): 103-23.

Williams, Leonard. "Political Advertising in the 'Year of the Woman': Did X Mark the Spot?" In Elizabeth Cook, Sue Thomas and Clyde Wilcox, eds., *The Year of the Woman: Myths and Realities,* 197-215. Boulder, CO: Westview Press, 1994.

"Women Candidates in 1996." In Center for the American Woman and Politics, Eagleton Institute of Politics, Rutgers University, *News and Notes* 11 (Summer 1996): 14-25.

"Women Make News As Voters, Edge Upward as Officeholders." In Center for the American Woman and Politics, Eagleton Institute of Politics, Rutgers University, *News and Notes* 11 (Spring 1997): 1.

Women's Campaign Fund promotional literature (1995).

"Women's Voices: Solutions for a New Economy." Report prepared by Lake Research for the Center for Policy Alternatives (Sept. 1996).

"Work Week." *Wall Street Journal,* 10 June 1997, 1.

"Work Week: Female Executives Score Well in Gender Study." *Wall Street Journal,* 24 September 1996, 1.

Yang, John E. "Political Parent Trap II." *Washington Post,* 30 June 1996, A8.

Index

Abrams, Robert, 58
Abzug, Bella, 59
Advertising, political, 139, 143-44
African American candidates, 62
Albright, Madeline, 95
Allen, George, 62
American Association of University Women (AAUW), 87, 127, 129, 138
Anderson, Karen, 51, 55, 70, 73, 104, 107-8, 118
Apter, Terri, 33, 53
Are, Lisa, 54-55, 103, 106, 150
Ashe, Kathy, 94, 97, 117, 139, 140, 144

Baer, Denise, 3
Baird, Zoe, 32, 103, 147
Banker's Trust Company (mentoring program), 49
Banking scandal (U.S. House of Representatives), 13
Baskerville, Viola, 22, 67, 74, 81, 102, 136
Becker, Vaneta, 52, 60, 71, 77, 96, 98
Bem, Sandra Lipsitz, 94
Berheide, Catherine White, 18
Biden, Joseph, 147
Bledsoe, Timothy, 74
Blevins, Patricia, 22, 77, 101, 121, 146, 147
Boscia, Jo Ann, 47, 53, 58, 72, 83, 97, 145

Braden, Maria, 140
Brown, George, 131
Browner, Carol, 32
Budak, Mary Kay, 24, 57, 77, 79, 101-2, 150
Burstein, Karen, 59
Business and Professional Women, 127
Businesswomen, 12, 16-18, 26, 72-73, 78, 80, 82, 95-96, 120

Cameron, Penny, 107, 118, 121, 129
Campaign ads, 143-44
Campaign fundraising. *See* Fundraising
Campaigning
  negative, 143-46
  skills needed for, 48
  by women, 10
Campaigns and Elections, 142
Carroll, Susan, 31, 67
Carter, Jimmy, 31
Carter, Mickii, 78, 81, 93, 100, 103, 127, 150
Catalyst (research organization), 78
Caucuses (women's), 97
Center for Policy Alternatives, 155
Center for Responsive Politics, 120
Center for the American Woman and Politics (Rutgers University), 8, 35, 37, 102, 104, 161
Child care, 22, 32, 63, 103
Chowdhury, Najma, 18

Cino, Maria, 115
Clinton, Bill, 32, 88, 153, 154
Clinton, Hillary, 103, 133
Coalition building, 152, 156
Collins, Susan, 155
Congress, U.S.
　male-female ratio in, 15
　number of women in, 1, 7, 8, 9, 13 (table)
　women candidates for, 15
Congressional Women, 76
Cooper, Shirley, 24-25, 37, 58, 71, 99

Dean, George, 157
The Deep Divide: Why American Women Resist Equality, 87
Democratic conventions, 115
Democratic National Committee, 115
Democratic party, 114, 115, 124, 155
Democratic women, 8, 97, 153. *See also* individual names
Dole, Bob, 88, 153, 154
Duff, Carolyn, 96
Dumdi, Ellie, 118, 140

Elections. *See* names of individual candidates
EMILY's List, 44-45, 60, 126
Environmental Protection Agency, 32
Equal Rights Amendment, 153

Fagan, Jim, 69
Family and Medical Leave Act, 8
Farmer, Nancy, 107
Feinstein, Dianne, 127, 141
Ferguson, Anita Perez, 95
Ferraro, Geraldine, 58-59, 62, 92
50/50 by 2000, 157
Florio, Jim, 62
Fowler, Tillie, 23
Friedenberg, Robert, 143

Fundraising
　comparisons among states (chart), 61
　male and female candidates compared, 60-61, 119-20
　by women politicians, 10-11, 59-62, 125, 126, 152

Gallese, Liz Roman, 73
Garamendi, Patricia, 30
Gender gap, 153-54
Gertzog, Irwin, 76
Gilligan, Carol, 137
Gingrich, Newt, 115
Ginsburg, Ruth Bader, 151
Giuliani, Rudy, 132
Glass ceiling, 16, 17-18
Glass Ceiling Commission (U.S. Department of Labor), 16
Goldberg, Jeffrey, 142
Goodman, Ellen, 58, 85-86
Government contracts, 120
Governorships, 1, 8
Greater Roles and Opportunities for Women (GROW), 126

Hamburg, Joan, 58
Hart, Bettieanne, 22, 25, 76, 134
Henry, Sherrye, 62-63, 87, 135
Herrick, Rebekah, 60
Herring, Mary, 74
Hill, Anita, 13, 140
Hoffman, Barbara, 67, 76
Holtzman, Elizabeth, 58-59
Hull, Jane Dee, 8
Hummer, Anita, 73, 76, 80, 99, 139
Hutchison, Kay Bailey, 24, 134, 151

Ibarra, Herminia, 78
Incumbency, 9, 14, 15, 86
International Women's Forum, 72
Inter-Parliamentary Union, 116
Irwin, Janet, 96

Jamieson, Kathleen Hall, 138
Jeruchim, Joan, 48, 51, 52
John, Susan, 51, 67-68, 72, 74, 93, 106-7, 119
Journalists, 140. *See also* Media
Junior League, 129

Kagan, Cheryl, 36, 53, 68, 74, 84
Kanter, Rosabeth, 46
Kelly, Sue, 36, 122
Kelso, Frank, 151
Kendrigan, Mary Lou, 115
Kifi, Faiza, 116
Klingler, Gwenn, 22, 23, 76, 84, 104-5, 116-17, 144
Knudson, Judy, 26, 71, 76-77, 92, 93, 137
Krahnke, Betty Ann, 71, 75, 81, 92, 144-45
Krasnow, Rose, 47

League of Women Voters, 41, 70, 87, 89, 90, 127, 128, 129
Lee, Marcia Manning, 26
Legislators' salaries, 69, 72
Levin, Susan Bass, 21, 34, 55, 79, 88, 101, 124-25, 126, 146
Lewis, Anthony, 147
Lincoln, Blanche Lambert, 30
Lobbyists, 77, 84
Lofgren, Zoe, 22-23
Lucas, L. Louise, 4, 36, 72, 75, 105-6, 127

Mahaffey, Maryann, 77-78
Make Women Count (MWC), 45, 127
Male politicians, 15, 46, 76, 80
Martynick, Karen
   on mentors and networking, 49, 55, 129-30
   on negative campaigning, 144
   on political parties' treatment of women politicians, 35, 117
   on politics and family life, 31
   on public image, 134
   on women party leaders, 125
   on women's solidarity, 41, 51
McCarthy, Colman, 59
McCarthy, Karen, 97
McKinney, Cynthia, 104
Media, 101, 133-34, 139, 140
Men and Women of the Corporation, 46
Mentors, 16, 17, 46-55, 76, 81-82
Messinger, Ruth, 132
Mezey, Susan Gluck, 34
Migden, Carole, 158
Miller, Karen, 120-21, 139-40, 146
Miller, Sandra, 31, 51-52, 59, 72, 75, 83, 106, 122-23, 125, 135
Mommy track, 29-39
Moore, Susanna, 133
Moseley-Braun, Carol, 142
Murray, Patty, 36, 122, 152
Myrick, Sue, 97

Nannygate, 32, 103
National Conference on State Legislatures, 9
National League of Cities, 47
National Organization for Women, 129
National Republican Congressional Committee, 115
National Women's Political Caucus (NWPC), 44, 95, 126
Nelson, Barbara, 18
Networking
   and businesswomen, 78, 82
   among politicians, 76, 129

O'Connor, Pamela, 57
Old boys' club, 46, 56-57, 76-82
Outlook (AAUW), 129

PAC's, 11, 44, 45, 60, 161-68 (list of)
Paglia, Camille, 133, 138
PAM's List, 126

Partisanship, 57
Paurrault, Michael, 96
Pell, Claiborne, 131
Pensions (public), 69
Peters, Rosemarie, 93, 96, 98, 100-101, 122, 130
Petersen, Eleanor, 17
Political Action Committees (PAC's), 11, 44, 45, 60, 161-68 (list of)
Political ads, 139, 143-44
Political parties
  and business, 112
  women leaders in, 123-25
  and women politicians, 7, 14, 35, 109, 111-30
  and women's affiliates, 126-27
Political power, 70-72
Politicians. *See* Women politicians and Male politicians and names of individuals
Politics
  and business, 119-21
  as a career, 66-69
  as warfare, 90, 92, 93-94, 138
Powers, Claudia, 25, 50, 67, 81-82
Presidential election, 1996 (chart), 153
Presley, Sue Ann, 134
Purnick, Joyce, 59

Reagan, Ronald, 31
Reno, Janet, 32
Republican conventions, 115, 123
Republican National Committee, 115
Republican party, 114, 115, 122, 124, 155
Republican Women of the 90's, 126
Republican women politicians, 8, 97, 153
Rich, Adrienne, 4
Richards, Ann, 89, 135, 150
Rosener, Judy B., 95-96

Rosin, Hanna, 142
Roth, Renee, 59
Roukema, Marge, 24

Safire, William, 43, 149
Salaries (of legislators), 9-10, 69, 72
Sanchez, Stephanie Hunter, 68
Sargent, Claire, 149
Savocchio, Joyce, 54, 102-3
Schenk, Lynn, 24
Schlenker, Alice, 22, 77, 116
Schneider, Claudine, 131
Schroeder, Patricia, 52, 133, 141
Schwartz, Felice, 30-31
Selin, Christina, 23, 68, 83-84
Sex discrimination, 18, 33-34, 53, 56, 103, 115-16
Sex-role stereotyping, 11, 82-86, 108-9
Sexual harassment, 151
Shaheen, Jeanne, 141
Shapiro, Pat, 48, 51, 52
Shaw, Judy Ferguson, 24, 54
Smith, Adele, 36, 54, 71, 72, 75, 108-9, 118, 145
Smith, Linda, 131
Smith, Mary L., 115
Snowe, Olympia, 123
State legislatures, 2, 7, 9, 10, 13 (table), 14, 46, 127-28
Steinem, Gloria, 59
Stereotyping, 11, 82-86, 108-9
Stewart, Mimi, 35, 36, 107, 117
Suffragist movement, 17
Supreme Court, 151
Symington, Fife, 8

Tackett, Michael, 154
Tailhook scandal, 151
Term limits, 86-87, 107, 158-59
Terry, Mary Sue, 30, 62

Thatcher, Margaret, 89
Thomas, Clarence, 13
Training seminars, 133, 139
Trent, Judith, 143

Vallance, Elizabeth, 18
Voter preferences, 62, 83
Voter registration, 87 (table)
Voters, 152-56
Voting by gender, 8, 149, 150, 151-52

Waldholtz, Enid Greene, 142, 150
Weaver, Marcia, 21, 99
Wellesley College Center for Research on Women, 80-81
Wentling, Rose Mary, 82
When Women Work Together, 96
Whitman, Christine Todd, 21, 62, 122, 127, 152
Wilde, Linda, 131
WISH List, 44, 45, 126
Women and Politics Worldwide, 18
Women attorneys, 12
Women candidates, 14-15, 38, 58-59, 60-63, 121
Women delegates, 115
Women governors, 1, 8
Women in business, 12, 16-18, 26, 72-73, 78, 80, 82, 95-96, 120
Women in Municipal Government, 47
Women in the Senate and House (WISH), 44, 45, 126
Women journalists, 140
Women mayors, 7
Women, Mentoring and Success, 48
Women politicians
  accessibility of, 98-102
  African American, 4
  ages of, 12
  alienation of, 18
  and ambition, 15-16, 38, 68
  author's interviews with, 3-4
  balancing career and family, 12, 19-25, 34, 47-48, 86, 108, 146-47
  compared with women in business, 17
  on credibility, 25, 81, 102-3, 133, 139-40
  crossing party lines, 97, 127, 151
  Democratic, 8, 97, 153
  diversity of perspectives among, 150-51
  education and experience of, 12, 35, 37, 104, 127-28
  emotions shown by, 141-42
  fundraising by, 10-11, 59-62, 125, 126, 152
  impact of incumbency on, 9, 14, 15, 86
  influence of, on male politicians, 80, 108
  influence on legislation, 7-8
  on lack of women candidates, 88, 121
  and leadership, 72, 75, 83, 97, 107, 124-25
  legislative priorities of, 21-22, 56, 74, 140
  on lobbyists, 77, 84
  and the media, 101, 133-34, 139, 140
  and mentors, 16, 17, 46-55, 76, 81-82
  and the "Mommy Track," 29-39
  motivations of, 15-16, 73
  on negative political environment, 144-46
  number of, 1-2, 8, 9, 13, 116
  obstacles to political advancement of, 12, 106-7
  occupations of, 12
  and "old boys' club," 76-77, 79, 118
  and party loyalty, 114, 119, 121-22

Women politicians *(continued)*
  perceptions of, 84-85, 92, 93
  physical appearance of, 48, 131-37, 147
  on political confrontations, 93, 96, 98, 100, 101, 122, 130
  on political effficacy, 75
  and political parties, 7, 14, 35, 109, 111-30
  on political power, 70, 71, 72, 74
  political strategies of, 79-80, 90-91, 99, 100, 104-5, 107-8
  on politics and business, 119
  and politics as a career, 66-69
  and public image, 48, 132-37
  public perceptions of, 7, 11, 27, 75, 98, 102, 104, 143-44, 147
  radio programs of, 80, 99, 106
  Republicans, 8, 97, 153
  and sex discrimination, 18, 33-34, 53, 56, 103, 115-16
  solidarity among, 41-59, 121-23, 126-27, 151
  speech and voices of, 137-41
  in state legislatures, 2, 7, 8, 9, 10, 13, 14, 127-28
  stereotyping of, 11, 82-86, 108-9
  training seminars for, 133, 139
  on women running against women, 57, 58-59
  and women's groups, 126-29
  and "women's issues," 84, 91, 102

Women Politicians and the Media, 140
Women, Politics and American Society, 115
Women voters, 152-56
Women-owned businesses, 120
Women's Campaign Research Fund, 44, 133, 139
Women's Campaign School (Yale University), 139
Women's caucuses, 8, 97
Women's groups, 126-29
"Women's issues," 84, 91, 102
Women's speech, 137-41
Wong, Martha, 56, 73, 79, 123, 125-26, 135-36, 139
Wood, Kimba, 32
Working Women Don't Have Wives, 33, 53

Yeakel, Lynn, 131
Year of the Woman
  fundraising in, 60
  lack of progress following, 2, 9, 13 (table), 14, 15
  media response to, 15
  numbers of women candidates in, 14, 15
  political ads during, 139
  women elected during, 1-2, 9, 13, 155

Zey, Michael, 78